"In *Imagining Abundance* Kerry Robinson invites us to accompany her on a holy journey as she takes us on a personalized journey through her life as a philanthropist and fundraiser. The result is an insightful book that is a must read for donors and fundraisers who want to explore the ways in which faith and spiritual values can inspire and inform transformative and thoughtful giving."

> William G. Enright
> Senior Fellow & Founding Director
> The Lake Institute on Faith & Giving
> Lilly Family School of Philanthropy
> Indiana University

"*Imagining Abundance* is a spectacular achievement. I'm not surprised—no one is more capable of writing it than Kerry Robinson. She has so well integrated faith and philanthropy throughout her own life. She reminds that 'to whom much is given, much is expected' (Luke 12:48). It will be an inspiration to all of us to be good stewards of what God has given—so abundantly."

> Thomas Groome
> Professor of Theology and Religious Education,
>   Boston College
> Author of *What Makes Us Catholic*

"This is an essential and instructive book—and at the same time, it is also deeply spiritual and inspiring. It will speak profoundly to anyone interested in the deeper call of vocation, and in achieving great impact for God's people and the common good. Kerry Robinson speaks from firsthand experience and keen understanding of the two interrelated worlds of philanthropy and fundraising."

> Alexia Kelley
> President and CEO, Foundations and Donors
>   Interested in Catholic Activities (FADICA)

"In a voice that radiates joy from every page, Kerry Robinson shows us that there is grace to be had on both sides of the asking/giving coin, that 'other-centeredness' can truly be a vocation, and that we needn't worry about always slicing the pie more thinly. We have the ingredients to make vastly larger, more nutritious ones. This book, *Imagining Abundance*, makes me proud to be in the fundraising business!"

> Craig J. Leach
> CEO, Graham-Pelton Consulting, Inc./
>   Collegium, Inc.

"Pope Francis tells us that there is only one mission and it is Jesus' mission. Kerry calls us to live that mission with great hope, enthusiasm, and joy in abundance. Everyone involved in development should read *Imagining Abundance*. It would be a perfect gift to share with a board of directors or trustees. It is well worth the read, but more importantly worth the conversations and ideas it will inspire."

> Sr. Georgette Lehmuth, OSF
> President and CEO
> National Catholic Development Conference

"*Imagining Abundance* is an autobiographical case study of one of the most impressive campaigns in history to build a vibrant Catholic campus ministry center at a major research university. Kerry Robinson knows development both as a member of a philanthropic foundation and as a chief development officer. Her account provides more than principles for effective fundraising; it provides a spirituality of development work. This is a must read for all involved in faith-based development."

> Gregory E. Sterling
> The Reverend Henry L. Slack Dean
> The Lillian Claus Professor of New Testament
> Yale Divinity School

"Not since Henri Nouwen's little book on the spirituality of fundraising have we been given a jewel like this book. Kerry Robinson weaves her own story—which includes her deep roots in the Raskob family's remarkable philanthropic spirit—together with priceless practical theological wisdom and marvelous examples of everyday people serving God and the church. By doing so with such candor and grace, Robinson helps us glimpse the Holy Spirit at work in our midst when we re-imagine philanthropy and fundraising as signs of the abundance that flow from the generosity of God."

> John Wimmer
> Program Director, Religion
> Lilly Endowment

IMAGINING ABUNDANCE

Fundraising, Philanthropy, and a Spiritual Call to Service

Kerry Alys Robinson

LITURGICAL PRESS

Collegeville, Minnesota

www.litpress.org

	5	6	7	8	9

Library of Congress Cataloging-in-Publication Data

Robinson, Kerry A.
　　Imagining abundance : fundraising, philanthropy, and a spiritual call to service / Kerry Alys Robinson.
　　　　pages　cm
　　ISBN 978-0-8146-3766-1　—　ISBN 978-0-8146-3791-3　(ebook)
　　　1. Catholic Church—Charities.　2. Church charities.　3. Service (Theology)　4. Generosity—Religious aspects—Christianity.
　　5. Christians—Charitable contributions.　6. Church fund raising　I. Title.

BX2347.R63　2014
262.0068'1—dc23
　　　　　　　　　　　　　　　　　　　　　　　　　　　　2014025292

"It's good to be blessed. It's better to be a blessing."

—unknown

"What we have done for ourselves alone dies with us; what we have done for others and the world remains and is immortal."

—Albert Pike

Contents

Acknowledgments

I have been inspired, challenged, encouraged, and ennobled by being part of the Raskob Foundation for Catholic Activities, FADICA (Foundations and Donors Interested in Catholic Activities), Saint Thomas More Catholic Chapel and Center at Yale University, and the National Leadership Roundtable on Church Management. I am indebted to all—past and present—who have created, led, served, and belonged to these communities: founders, trustees, staff, members, and benefactors. For their invaluable lessons in faith, generosity, service, perseverance, compassion, and vision, and for making this a better church and world, I am grateful.

Thank you to Fr. T. Lawrason Riggs, John and Helena Raskob, and Geoffrey T. Boisi, visionary founders with remarkable conviction, generosity, prescience, fortitude, and integrity.

Thank you to the members of my wide, extended families: the Robinsons, Cappellos, Loftins, and Raskobs. Every day I learn from them and cannot imagine how impoverished my life would be without belonging to them.

Thank you to Tom Groome, Jake Schrum, Paul Butler, Michael O'Loughlin, Theresa Robinson, Martha Whitfield, Mary Ann Wasil, Margie Clark, Unmesh Brahme, John Wimmer, Curtis Beavers, and Nate Short for encouraging me to write.

Thank you to the editors and staff of Liturgical Press for unwittingly making a dream come true by surprising me with a book contract and asking me to sign it.

Thank you to Sr. Eileen Dooling, RSM, and the staff at Mercy Center in Madison, Connecticut, for offering me a chance to write from the room by the water where Henri Nouwen wrote. Thank you to the pastoral team at Saint Thomas More Catholic Chapel and Center at Yale for making the entire Golden Center available to me at night and on the weekends to complete this manuscript. I cannot think of more inspiring settings or more welcoming hosts. And to Henri Nouwen and Tom Golden whose lives were such a blessing and whose friendship and inspiration remain a constant source of encouragement even in death—thank you.

Thank you to Fr. Joe Donnelly, Fr. Ron Rolheiser, OMI, and Sr. Margaret Farley, RSM, for teaching me about faith through their words and example, caring for my spiritual health and development, and above all for their friendship.

Thank you to my father, Peter S. Robinson, to Mary Ellen O'Driscoll, and to Monica Kennedy DeBenedet for absolutely insisting that I never give up on the capital campaign.

Thank you to Amy McClenning who joined the pastoral team at Saint Thomas More Chapel on my birthday sixteen years ago and from that day forward has been a constant, cherished gift. For all of her encouragement, humor, compassion, empathy, support, perspective, and love I will always be grateful.

Thank you to Fr. Bob Beloin, consummate priest, invaluable colleague, indelible friend.

Thank you to my parents, Ann and Peter Robinson, to my brother Peter, and to my sister-in law Theresa. I am grateful every day for the countless ways they bless my life.

Thank you to my children, Christopher and Sophie, for reminding me that a champagne book tour is fine, but the book needs to be written first, and for being the specific daily reason my heart is full of gladness.

Thank you to my husband, Michael Cappello, who does everything with excellence and total dedication, whose support is unwavering, whose love is constant, and whose commitment to making this a better world is appreciated in our home and across the globe.

Introduction

Imagine that you have the ability to transform your organization.

Imagine being able to advance the mission of your charitable nonprofit to unprecedented effect. Picture yourself as an agent of change for your faith community bringing to full fruition what most think is impossible. Imagine that as a consequence of your dedication, your ministry reaches more people than you will ever fully realize, providing them hope, encouragement, and help. Imagine that your nonprofit is financially healthy, well-respected, and carried forward with excellence at every level.

What would you need to have such an impact?

Many in the world see limitation, scarcity, insurmountable obstacles, and inability, while yearning for the opposite.

There is no magic wand, no secret formula, no set of perfect preconditions for profound positive impact. Yet everyone can be an agent of transformation.

You can be an agent of transformation. You have everything at your disposal right now to advance your organization's mission, to raise money, to equip your ministry to be profoundly beneficial to others.

My guess, and the reason for this book, is that you are not yet fully aware of all that you have at your disposal to play such a meaningful role in the life of your organization or community. And whether you are the pastor, provincial, bishop, executive director, development director, trustee, founder, benefactor, program officer, or advocate of your organization, you can be extraordinarily effective.

If, by virtue of your role, you have been given a mandate to be part of the new life of the organization or to advance the mission but don't know where to start, or doubt your ability to be effective, or hate the idea of raising money, this book is for you. You and the ministries and missions you value that are oriented toward making this a better world for others are the reason this book was written.

There is a very old folktale that has been passed through the generations. So sweetly entertaining to children and adults alike is this tale, of which there are many versions, that the powerful moral of the story is nearly always overlooked. It centers on a single person, a stranger, who happens upon a village. The stranger is hungry and thirsty; the villagers are timid, afraid, isolated in their impoverishment. There is a stultifying air to the community. Everyone is reserved; there is little vitality. A pall is cast upon the village. When the stranger gently inquires if there is food that can be shared with her, she is met with blank stares, fear, embarrassment, and regret. Gently prodding, she is told of the pervasive scarcity in the village. The villagers simply have nothing to offer. Each has only enough and barely enough for his or her own family.

> "Start by doing what is necessary; then do what's possible; and suddenly you are doing the impossible."
>
> —St. Francis of Assisi

The stranger changes everything. She announces that she has what the community needs: a special stone. The stone has the power to create a spectacular, succulent, nourishing soup. The villagers do not believe her, but she persists. So enthusiastically does she speak of the power of the special stone, so vividly does she describe the aroma and taste of the soup that soon some of the villagers become curious. She entreats the villagers to experience the power of the special stone and to see for themselves. She asks, "Surely there is someone who has a large pot in this village. And surely someone in the village has enough water to nearly fill the pot." One villager, figuring there was nothing to lose by lending his pot, retreats to procure it for the soup, and another, skeptically, offers to fetch water. Now with water and a pot, the stranger takes great care to drop the special stone in it. A fire is lit beneath the pot, and the stranger stirs the water and stone with great reverence. "Carrots and potatoes would go very well with this stone soup, if anyone in the village happens to have any," she suggests. Carrots and potatoes are soon added, and as the soup is stirred and excitement grows, other villagers begin to volunteer ideas for additional ingredients. Beans and spices, herbs, tomatoes and corn are gathered from villagers' homes and brought for the communal soup. Before too long everyone is participating, volunteering to contribute something to add, and when the pot begins to overflow, villagers bring out other offerings. They set up tables and chairs and gather plates and silverware, napkins, glasses, flowers, bread, and wine. Excitement grows all the while the stranger stirs the soup with the special stone and encourages and invites everyone to participate. And at last the soup is ready, the table is laid, and there is an abundant feast for all in the village.

This book is for you. You are the one in possession of the stone.

1

Two Sides of a Philanthropic Coin

Seventy years ago, our great grandparents John and Helena Raskob established a private family foundation with two expressed intentions: they wanted all of the foundation's resources to be used exclusively to support the activities, apostolates, and ministries of the Catholic Church throughout the world, and they wanted their children and descendants to be stewards of the foundation's resources.

Sounds simple enough until one considers that being open to any activity, apostolate, or ministry of the Catholic Church anywhere in the world hardly narrows or focuses the field of philanthropic opportunity. Compounding the challenge, John and Helena had thirteen children, one of whom, our grandmother, had fourteen children. Our family has grown exponentially. Invitations are extended upon family members reaching the age of eighteen; the fifth generation is now well represented in formal membership. All participation is voluntary, non-remunerative, and understood to be a serious commitment of time, focus, and engagement in the life of the church.

Today there are nearly one hundred members, all descendants of John and Helena, actively engaged in the work of the foundation, making site visits, reviewing proposals, and meeting to determine which applicants would most benefit from the foundation's resources. It has been an uncommon privilege to serve the church in this way, with the unanticipated, beneficial consequence of evangelization for our family. Our faith lives are stronger because we have had the opportunity to meet, learn from, and support some of the most inspiring, generous, compassionate, effective people the church has to offer. These women and men, ordained, religious, and lay, offer a broken world hope by extending mercy, alleviating suffering, educating children, providing catechesis, championing justice, advancing peace, healing the sick, and reducing poverty.

> "I have found that among its other benefits, giving liberates the soul of the giver."
>
> —Maya Angelou

Our applicants are more than deserving grantees; they are role models. They restore our faith in the church and in humankind. It is a humbling privilege to play even a tiny role in their lives by directing foundation resources to their ministries. As children and young adults we marveled at their example and wondered how they could daily encounter so much human suffering and inequality and yet possess a palpable sense of joy and purpose. Grounded in deep spirituality and prayer, profoundly self-aware and other-centered, able to see God so readily in others, especially the poor, they were deeply compelling role models.

As children, we wanted to be like them but presumed we could never be so selfless, so holy. We prayed to do something with our lives that would have a beneficial effect on their lives, our moral heroines and heroes. If we couldn't *be* one of them, perhaps we could support them with full intention, helping to make their ministries even more effective, less burdened. Maybe then our lives, by extension, would be imbued with purpose, too.

Flowers with Care

As young members of the foundation, we were captivated by one particular grantee. The story went as follows:

A newly ordained priest was assigned by his bishop to work within the juvenile justice system and minister to young adults who were incarcerated. It was tremendously difficult, often emotionally wrenching, dispiriting work. Every day he would visit the prison to meet with the young adults and extend consoling words of encouragement and hope. Nothing he did or said seemed to make any difference in the gulf of despondence, regret, anger, resentment, and apathy his young charges expressed. It all seemed so hopeless, so futile, and the young priest, himself, was close to despair.

He sought help, spoke to his spiritual director, and took it all to prayer. And he didn't walk away. All these kids needed, he figured, was one more adult giving up on them. What he wanted was the ability to provide a horizon for them, something that would give them a reason to have hope, hope in a future that would be better than the misery of their incarceration. It wasn't enough to convey that they would soon be released from prison because they knew the high percentage of recidivism, and, worse, they knew what daily life on the outside entailed for them.

So he set about figuring out what would break the cycle of poverty, violence, bad choices, and despair.

An idea surfaced, a possibility to consider. As improbable as it seemed, it surely had merit because it was an idea that was born of other-centered, loving intention. The idea was full of potential but would take enormous work. The young priest set out to visit all of the local, mom- and pop-owned flower shops in the metropolitan area. He shared his predicament, his ministerial assignment, and how hard it had been in the absence of anything concretely hopeful to offer the young adults in prison. He spoke of the goodness and dignity he saw in each of them, of the potential he knew was their birthright. He described his idea for a novel intervention and asked them to be part of it. The idea was this: each flower store owner was asked to participate in a new ministry and serve as a mentor to one of the young adults upon his or her release from prison. The young adult would serve as an apprentice, learning everything about the flower trade and flower arrangement craft as possible under the tutelage of the owner and staff. The young adult would agree to work in the flower shop, and stipends would be provided through the fundraising the young priest would do to support this ministry. At first there was skepticism and foreboding. The priest persisted and persuaded, and soon the first few owners agreed to participate. And soon a few more agreed, and the fear dissipated, and the skepticism was put aside, and before long the priest had enough shops for every young adult.

What was the outcome? Imagine you are celebrating the birthday of a dear friend or relative. You stop in at your local florist to place an order and discuss how much you are interested in spending, what kind of flowers you would most like, and other details. You continue to run errands and return to pick up the flower arrangement at a later time in the day. When you walk into the shop, you let the shop staff know that you are here to pick up an order. The young apprentice goes into the back of the shop to retrieve the arrangement, brings it to you, and the very first thing you are likely to say is, "That is beautiful. Thank you."

> "Real generosity toward the future lies in giving all to the present."
>
> —Albert Camus

For many of these young adults, it was the first time anyone had ever told them that something they created was beautiful. The positive affirmation and genuine gratitude continued with every order. Over time this had a beneficial effect on the self-esteem of these previously demoralized young adults. Now they had a marketable skill, a craft, an income, role models and mentors, affirmation, and beauty on a daily basis. And they had someone who believed in them. The flower store owners and staff who participated in the mentoring effort reported greater levels of meaning in their own work, customers who knew of the program wanted to increase their patronage of participating shops, and donors were grateful to be part of something life-giving. Everybody benefited.

Here was an example of a person of faith who didn't just want to care for what had been entrusted to him; he saw potential and acted on it, and he gave everything he had to bring that potential to fruition.

Maximizing the Impact of the Grant Dollar

I was not quite ten years old when my father, Peter S. Robinson, was appointed the first president of FADICA (Foundations and

Donors Interested in Catholic Activities), a remarkable consortium of Catholic philanthropic foundations whose members and trustees intuitively knew that shared knowledge and collaboration would strengthen the efficacy of their individual grant-making and set the stage for greater potential collective impact. The Raskob Foundation was one of several founding members of FADICA. FADICA was an intriguing idea born of the desire to be even more effective in philanthropic mission, to be an even more effective steward of entrusted resources. Our relatives, active in the Raskob Foundation at the time, observed that many of their most inspiring grantees were indicating that they were receiving additional grant support from several other notable family foundations. It made sense to these families that they meet to explore how they could be mutually supportive in a shared mission, that is, philanthropically supporting the Catholic Church and faith-based ministries. For the members of the Raskob family and foundation, this was a specific opportunity to be an even greater steward of the resources that had been entrusted to us by John and Helena Raskob.

It was an immediate success, and over time the consortium grew. Although my father served as founding president and catalyst, he is famous for saying that the greatest contribution he made to FADICA was finding his successor, Francis J. Butler, whose leadership spanned three decades, whose contribution to the church cannot be measured, and who became one of my most important mentors in the world of philanthropy.

Members of FADICA meet to inform themselves of the pressing needs facing the church, the better to anticipate how they can meet those challenges efficaciously through their philanthropy. My uncle, Charles Raskob Robinson, who served on the board of FADICA representing the Raskob Foundation for many years, always spoke of the importance of "following the vibrancy." What he meant by this was that those individual leaders—ordained, religious, or lay—possessed a combination of insight, courage, passion, fortitude, and integrity that engendered confidence in the grant maker. Identifying the "vibrancy" meant a funder could take a risk on supporting a seemingly wild idea, because the leader had established a track record of getting the job done, demonstrating keen prophetic insight, sticking with the effort, and commanding respect. FADICA provided a venue for funders to meet such leaders in the church and faith-based ministries, to learn from thought leaders and each other, and to cultivate the art of recognizing potential the better to act on it.

The FADICA experiment met the test of win-win-win. It was not only the members of FADICA who benefited from greater knowledge, shared best practices in the mechanics of philanthropy, and new opportunities to maximize the grant dollar. Grantees also benefited. It is far more advantageous for a grantee to receive $250,000 from five separate, credible foundations than to receive the same amount from only one. Investment by multiple funders in a charitable cause establishes legitimacy and sets the stage for ongoing relationships between the funders and grantee. And while we were never excused from conducting our own due diligence in evaluating a grant opportunity for Raskob, it added to our measure of confidence when one of our respected partners in FADICA was already on record as supporting the grantee.

"My mother taught me that to maximize your philanthropic potential, you need to constantly challenge your capabilities and put yourself in situations that are not always comfortable. Through her example, I discovered that there is no more beautiful way to live a life than to live a life of service."

—Laura Arrillaga-Andreessen

FADICA has provided the occasion to meet exceptional and visionary philanthropists, including strong women who lead their families' philanthropy and, from my earliest memories, championed the importance of meaningful roles of leadership for women in the church and in the world.

The best philanthropists are looking for the best opportunities to invest for the greatest return. And the return in philanthropy is impact. A dazzling example of the beneficial outcome of dedicated, faith-filled, tenacious, smart, and mission-driven leaders working together is the Cristo Rey Network. The world is better for the friendship of Fr. John Foley, SJ, and B. J. and Bebe Cassin.

In 1996 Fr. Foley founded the very first Cristo Rey college preparatory high school in Chicago for students whose families had few if any options to provide quality education for their children. What was particularly ingenious was the innovative business model built into the concept. Since this was a private Jesuit Catholic high school for children living below the poverty line, there would be no revenue from tuition. Ensuring the sustainability of this lifeline out of poverty for Cristo Rey's students was essential. The solution came in the form of partnerships with local businesses. School days are extended at Cristo Rey, during which meals are also provided. Every high school student at Cristo Rey works one day a week at a local law firm or business, essentially sharing a full-time position with four other classmates, each assigned to a different day of the week. The compensation goes directly to the school to offset tuition costs.

Much like Flowers with Care, the benefit was far more than merely economic. The personal relationships that are developed are deeply meaningful and often extend beyond high school. Students were assigned to places of employment in parts of Chicago they had never been to before, they rode on elevators in skyscrapers for the first time in their lives, they were being exposed to a business environment whose full-time employees quickly became the students' champions, and everyone's consciousness was expanded. Cristo Rey properly boasts an exceptionally high graduation and college matriculation rate. It is a success story from every perspective. And it was the comprehensive thoughtfulness of so many details, coupled with passion for a deeply important and urgent mission, that attracted B. J. and Bebe Cassin's interest.

B. J. is the founder of the Cassin Educational Initiative Foundation dedicated to establishing quality Catholic middle and high schools in economically challenged communities and is credited with providing both the intellectual capital and the initial philanthropic capital to take the Cristo Rey model and expand it nationwide. The Cassins did not merely make a grant, they brought their experience, their intellectual capabilities, their social capital, and their fine business acumen to the equation. Their involvement and investment helped to attract the interest and subsequent financial support of the Gates Foundation. Today twenty-five Cristo Rey Network high schools and sixty-four Nativity Miguel Network middle schools enroll more than 12,390 students. The schools serve only economically disadvantaged students.

Fr. Foley and B. J. and Bebe are heroes to us and to thousands of children. They saw potential and acted upon it, refusing to give up until it was a success. And when we thank them or tell them how much we marvel at what exemplary stewards they are, what is their response? Total humility. They deflect the compliment and light up as they begin to talk about the extraordinary young adults who are the pride and joy of the Cristo Rey alumni network.

From Philanthropy to Fundraising

I would have been content to dedicate my entire professional life to the activity of philanthropy, helping funders and foundations make sound investments in people and social enterprises. Philanthropy sounds easy, even luxurious, but anyone who has ever attended to philanthropy seriously knows how demanding and exacting it can be. There are inherently limited resources to extend, always more opportunity and need than available dollars to offer. Consequently the dominant challenge for the dedicated philanthropist is to be strategic, set priorities, exercise effective due diligence, maximize the impact of the grant dollar, and measure impact. No easy feat, made all the more difficult by having to turn down inherently worthy proposals and applicants, in favor of those that will be funded. Yet even so, I vastly preferred the role of grant maker to its corollary: fundraiser. All of that changed the day I found myself cast in a most unlikely role: director of development for Saint Thomas More Catholic Chapel and Center at Yale University, charged with leading a multimillion-dollar capital campaign.

In the summer of 1997 I received a call from Fr. Robert L. Beloin, the Catholic chaplain at Yale University. He told me that he was concluding his third year at Yale and had persuaded his predominantly lay board to embark upon a professional development effort to benefit Catholic campus ministry at the university. The goal was $5 million to be raised over five years. The position was envisioned to be part-time, low stress, entail very little travel, and could be evaluated on a year-to-year basis. One million dollars was intended for a 3,000-square-foot student center to be built adjacent to the existing Catholic chapel, and $4 million was earmarked for endowment. (When Fr. Bob first made this proposal, a trustee opined that he agreed a capital campaign was needed, but he thought the goal should be $1 million, and he doubted whether even that amount could be raised.) Fr. Bob explained that the board had advised that fundraising companies be considered, that several representatives from these companies had been interviewed but none presented an affordable, personal match that would work. A trustee had then generously recused herself from the board and volunteered to serve as the development director in a part-time capacity. A few months later, however, the trustee accepted a full-time position out of state and had to resign, which brought Fr. Bob to this point. He worried about losing his board's enthusiasm for the campaign. And there was the matter that no money had been raised yet. I listened patiently, accustomed to calls that were often appeals for advice on how to obtain grant support or which foundations to approach. When I asked Fr. Bob how he thought I might be helpful, he replied, "I would like you to be the director of development and lead this capital campaign." He paused and then added, "Your name came to me in prayer."

> "If you want to make God laugh, tell God about your plans."
>
> —Woody Allen

Perhaps the best development pickup line I have ever heard.

But there was no way I was going to assent to his request. I hated the very thought of fundraising. I couldn't imagine being responsible for directing a major campaign. I was wholly untrained in fundraising, admitted to terrible biases about the activity of fundraising, and assumed it would be arduous, thankless work. I had not so much as been entrusted to serve at a bake sale for our toddler's daycare. And then there was the practical matter that I was pregnant with our second child, and my plans were laid out quite clearly and cozily and centered on quiet domestic bliss.

I took a deep breath and began to prepare Fr. Bob for my gentle declination of his kind and flattering, if wholly misguided, invitation: "Thank you for thinking of me. I am honored. I should let you know that I am pregnant with my second child."

Long silence on the phone.

I waited. And waited. And then came a surprisingly enthusiastic response, "Congratulations! Wonderful news! Very happy for you. You can work from home."

In the space it took for me to realize what had just happened, Fr. Bob filled the void, "Kerry, please don't give me your answer now. All I ask is that you pray about this for five days and then call me. Whatever your answer is after five days of prayer, I will of course accept and respect it."

And what do you do with a request like that? If you are like me, you readily agree, knowing that after five days of prayer your "no" will be especially eloquent and gracious.

Five days later, I called Fr. Bob with my reply. And even today, seventeen years later, as I write this chapter for a book that was commissioned about the spirituality of philanthropy *and* fundraising, I am both astonished and deeply grateful that I found myself saying, "Yes."

What Happened in Prayer

What happened in prayer was the realization that this was not fundamentally a job offer to raise money but an invitation to work with an exceptional priest, pastor, and chaplain, to help bring to fruition a Catholic intellectual and spiritual center of consequence at one of the world's great universities. He was not offering me a job but a chance to live out my vocation. And, furthermore, the success of the effort would not be measured by Yale having one more thing to be properly proud of, but rather, by the positive impact such an example of vibrant, innovative campus ministry would have on the whole field of Catholic campus ministry nationally. From the very beginning days of prayer, a dominant motivation for pouring ourselves into this effort was to elevate Catholic campus ministry nationally, extend hope to campus ministers, expand the programmatic imagination, highlight the possibilities at hand, and present an irresistible and concrete example as a viable beacon.

On one hand, it may seem that philanthropy—giving away money to support worthy projects and ministries—and fundraising—asking for money to support worthy projects and ministries—are diametrically opposite fields of endeavor. Having spent decades in each pursuit I am convinced they are interrelated, necessary corollaries. They are elegantly two sides of a charitable coin. And most of us are both grant makers and grant seekers simultaneously throughout our lives.

In fact, the more seriously we live out our faith, the clearer the call to be generous and to live lives that inspire generosity. No one is excused from the responsibility and invitation to be generous and other-centered.

I have long believed that the whole religious and nonprofit sector would be more effective and less misunderstood if philanthropists and development officers had the chance to complete internships in each other's field of experience. It is far harder to exercise effective philanthropy than development officers sometimes understand, and it is far harder to lead successful development efforts than philanthropists sometimes understand. The most inspiring, effective, impactful, and noteworthy examples of excellent philanthropy and development share common characteristics. And this is especially true in the context of religious philanthropy and faith-based ministries.

> "Be who God meant you to be and you will set the world on fire."
> —St. Catherine of Siena

Philanthropy and development, when done faithfully and well, invite people into a relationship of common purpose, fulfill a noble purpose, point to meaning and transcendence, offer hope, and contribute to the lives of others, often those in great need. Both demand a radical generosity of spirit, time, effort, money, faith, tenacity, and conviction. One is not possible without the other. Both require a relinquishing of self, a disposition of humility before the great potential at hand, and the shared goal of blessing other people's lives.

On Generosity

We mistakenly assume philanthropy is the provenance of the very wealthy. This lets the rest of us off the hook. But a core tenet of faith is the call to live lives of authenticity, honesty, vulnerability, and generosity. Central to Christianity is the conviction that one finds life by giving it first away. Generosity, other-centeredness, mercy, compassion, relinquishment: these are constitutive qualities of being Christlike. Everyone has something to give others. We do a profound disservice to most of the world and to ourselves when we relegate philanthropy and giving only to the domain of the very wealthy.

A favorite story attributed to Mother Teresa takes place at a food-dispensing center in the midst of great poverty and hunger. One member of every family in the impoverished village would line up with a single bucket patiently waiting their turn to have the religious sisters fill their bucket with dry grains of rice. A novice was shadowing Mother Teresa as she methodically greeted each person and filled each bucket. Before long an elderly woman reached the front of the line and, to the novice's surprise, had in her possession two buckets.

> "Only a life lived for others is a life worthwhile."
>
> —Albert Einstein

Mother Teresa greeted her by name and proceeded to fill one bucket. After thanking Mother Teresa, the woman turned to leave, stopping a short distance later to empty half of her full bucket into the second empty bucket. The novice, miserable as a witness to the extent of the pervasive hunger and inequity, turned to Mother Teresa and asked, "Why did we not fill up both buckets for that poor elderly woman?" Mother Teresa replied, "There is only enough rice for each family to receive one bucket each day. She has her neighbors' bucket and her own. Her neighbors are very ill, and no one from the family could come to collect the rice. She is emptying half of her family's share into her neighbors' bucket to bring to them because she cannot carry more." Overwhelmed with sorrow, the novice demanded, "Surely we should fill both buckets and take the second bucket to the sick family for her." Mother Teresa stopped what she was doing and admonished the novice. "These are among the poorest and most destitute people you will ever meet. Never take away the right of another person to be generous."

Obstacles to Development

Right from the start, what struck me was the sheer volume of obstacles to successful development, beginning with my own shameful biases about the profession and wanton ignorance.

What are some of these obstacles?

The first observation has to do with language and the words we frequently use when discussing fundraising. Consider the following:

"Hit him up for money."

"Put the squeeze on her."

"Strong-arm him."

"Target them."

This is the language of violence and violation, not ministry and service.

And then there are the ironic intended compliments for the successful fundraiser: "Hold on to your wallet, here she comes! This is gonna cost you!" Or my personal favorite, said about me in my presence, "She's a pit bull when it comes to raising money. She'll take a bite out of your pant leg and get some flesh with it." What???????

Sometimes fundraising is cavalierly referred to as begging. Fundraising understood as begging places the fund seeker in a locus of scarcity, seeking alms. If, on the other hand, the fund seeker is fully cognizant of the abundant potential at hand and knows how much an investment would matter, for the beneficiary and the benefactor, then the request for financial support is not begging but invitation.

And there are fundraisers who inadvertently speak disparagingly about wealthy prospective donors. Perhaps it is sensitivity on my part having met so many deeply thoughtful, caring, exceedingly generous, and humble philanthropists, but I bristle at the ignorance and condescension when I hear, "He has so much money he doesn't even know what to do with it!"

We need to be careful with our language. Eliciting generosity and responding generously deserve reverence, not disparagement.

Second, there seems to be theological ambivalence about money. Is it holy, or is it sinful? If it is holy, is it only under prescribed circumstances? Perhaps wealth is neutral, and what is sinful or holy is how it is obtained, or the degree to which we are attached to it, or how we utilize it. Being aware of the theological ambivalence of wealth is a crucial first step to mitigating the cognitive dissonance one would otherwise bring to the task of religious fundraising.

Third, many faith leaders, especially religious and ordained, have received very little training in management, finances, and human resource development and even less training in fundraising and financial accountability and planning. We do not readily embrace responsibilities for which we have not been trained. The tasks then seem overwhelming and beyond our ken. When I speak about fundraising, I frequently begin by posing a single question to members of the audience, an audience often comprised of very accomplished leaders of faith. I ask them what thought or feeling is evoked when they hear me say, "As ministers, priests, religious, and lay leaders of faith-based nonprofits, you are responsible for the financial health of your community, parish, ministry, hospital, school, or nonprofit organization. Even if you have the luxury of a professional director of development, you are responsible for raising money to advance the mission of your organization."

"Success is to be measured not so much by the position that one has reached in life as by the obstacles which he has overcome while trying to succeed."

—Booker T. Washington

The answers are overwhelmingly fraught with anxiety and dread. "I know I have to do it, but regard it as a necessary evil." "I am more of a people person, so I really don't enjoy raising money or even discussing it." "Someone has to do it." "I feel dread, panic, a sense of futility." "Where to start?" "I really hate having to ask people for money." "I worry that I will never be able to raise enough money, fast enough, and people will be disappointed." "It makes me feel like I am using people, people I respect and would prefer to have as friends, not donors." "It makes me feel intensely pressured." "I bring a real heavy-heartedness to it and find I avoid it." "Terrified!"

And there are those leaders who insist it is not their job but the job of the development director or parishioners. The subtext of this conviction is that fundraising belongs to people not as important in the hierarchy as I am.

Fourth, many men and women have confided that they did not discern a vocation to the priesthood or religious life to make people uncomfortable by bringing up the unpleasant subject of money. They discerned their vocation to bring solace to others, to bring the Good News to others, to bring Christ to others. Intellectually they knew that in order for their ministries to thrive, they needed to be successful at fundraising, but this felt like too great a distraction—even a contradiction to their real ministry.

Development directors often are made to feel outside of the pastoral team for precisely this false logic. Their primary role is often, unfairly and incorrectly, understood as a business responsibility rather than a pastoral priority. The development director is categorized as being principally focused on money and transactions, not people and ministry. Not only does this do a profound disservice to development directors, it relegates fundraising to the periphery and falsely absolves other members of the pastoral team or nonprofit staff from having to be engaged, supportive, and responsible themselves. Soon an unspoken hierarchy of value is at hand, with fundraising lowest and staff who provide pastoral ministry compartmentalizing fundraising as beneath them. That development directors are often paid more than chaplains or pastoral associates only exacerbates this tension and confusion.

Fifth, there is a tremendous unease about having to ask people for favors. The assumption here is that in asking someone for a financial donation to support a ministry or a parish community, one is actually asking for a personal favor. The sense of having to owe the donor is unsettling, and to counteract this the discussion is framed in terms of obligation rather than invitation. Obligatory giving or giving out of guilt always signals a poor and ineffective development effort.

Sixth, compounding this unhelpful framework is the overwhelming fear of rejection and failure: What if the donor says no? Is that a rejection of my ministry, my priesthood, and my leadership? Is that a rejection of me?

Seventh, there is a way to comport oneself in the activity of fundraising that contributes to the biases many people have that it is slightly manipulative work, not fully transparent, somewhat deceiving, even sycophantic. Treating affluent and influential people with greater respect and dignity than those one believes can do little or nothing for you is not only a poor development practice, it is unfaithful and boorish. Integrity can never be sacrificed for development efficiency.

Here is my confession: I shared nearly all of these biases, fears, anxieties, suspicions, and misperceptions about fundraising, and if you, reading this, identify with any or all of these, this book is most certainly for you. My hope is to take all of those doubts, discomforts, and fears and persuade you that you do not need to be afraid because the premise that is giving rise to otherwise legitimate fears is a false premise. And what you have in your possession, what you have already been trained for, formed in, practice routinely, desire to grow in . . . these are the necessary ingredients to be successful at development. It is faith, spiritual maturation, desire to grow into the person you are meant to be, mercy, other-centered compassion, a commitment to the dignity of the human person, a zest for life and all that life has to offer, a belief in transcendence, access to hope, tenacity, humility, awe, generosity of spirit, joy, and the divine ability to imagine abundance that will be the hallmarks of your extraordinary success in fundraising, in philanthropy, and in service.

On Confronting Fear

Fear is the antithesis of faith. Scripture is filled with admonishments to "be not afraid." It is a core scriptural tenet: Fear not. Fear is useless; what is needed is trust.

The task of raising money—any amount of money—can seem so arduous, so impossible, so fraught with reasons for failure, so scary a task that rare is the leader or development officer who is unafraid. Reflect on the nature of your fear. What is it specifically that is informing your anxiety? Common answers to this question have included "I am afraid of failing." "I am afraid people will say no." "I am afraid that I will offend someone by asking for too much, or not enough."

"People of faith are confident in the future."

—Giuseppe Pittau, SJ

"I am afraid that I will let down my board, past donors, the constituencies our ministry serves." "I am afraid that I can't control the pace at which money will be raised." "I am afraid of the volume and magnitude of responsibility." "I am afraid to look foolish." "I am afraid to ask for help." "I am afraid to make the ask." "I am afraid that I will have only one chance to make the ask, and if I screw it up, I will have ruined the opportunity forever."

I will never forget meeting Robin Golden, the wonderfully successful director of development for Jewish life at Yale. With Rabbi James Ponet, she had expanded Jewish life on Yale's campus in a remarkable way, showing Yale faculty, students, officers, and alumni what a vibrant religious center on campus could look like. We were in their slipstream and eager to learn from them. Rabbi Ponet and Robin had completed their campaign and built the Slifka Center for Jewish life at Yale on Wall Street in New Haven and kindly gave Fr. Bob and me a tour of their beautiful facilities. I was enchanted, daunted, mesmerized, inspired, hopeful, and very, very afraid. At the end of our visit, I pulled Robin aside and I asked her quietly, "Robin, what if we are not successful at raising the money?"

Robin stopped walking, looked at me with serious intent, and said, "You can never allow yourself to ever entertain that question, ever again. That has to be the very last time you ever give voice to that question or that possibility. Decide right now that you will succeed, and never look back and question your capability again."

Fifteen years after Robin seared this into my consciousness, I had occasion to see her again at a retirement party for Rabbi Ponet. I reminded her of the conversation and her advice and thanked her for the exceptionally valuable wisdom she gave me that day. As Henry Ford said, "Whether you think you can, or you think you can't—you're right."

On Confronting Cynicism

One of the hardest realities one will confront is pervasive and insidious cynicism. Consequently, one of the most important characteristics a leader or development director must have is a palpable confidence and unshakeable faith that the potential can be brought to fruition. This confidence, this joyful expectation, this determination will be tested at every turn, definitely in the beginning, often in the face of new and novel possibilities, most certainly when the campaign in fact begins to be successful, and especially when change is occurring, and the stakes get higher, and much investment has already been placed in the effort.

"I would rather be a huge part of the problem than a small part of the solution."

—*The New Yorker* cartoon

It is hard to predict who will be the most difficult cynics, but you can absolutely count on the reality that you will swim in a sea of cynicism. It will be of paramount importance that you attend daily to prayer and reflection, examining anew that your intentions are sound, getting to the root of your motivations for working hard toward worthy goals and a vision of a better future for others. Make sure to stay focused on mission. Hold the future beneficiaries—people you may never meet, in your mind's eye. Be as other-centered and noble of purpose as possible. Reflect, pray, surrender, and ask for the grace to remain faithful to the task at hand. Hold the end—where the whole effort is heading—in mind. Think big. Remind yourself you only have this one life to live. Make it count. If you are prepared to work this devotedly, often dedicating many years, you might as well do it for maximum effect, do it right the first time, and aim for as close to perfect as possible.

Do not give in to the insidious temptation to acquiesce to cynicism even when it is proffered by smart, capable people you otherwise admire. Do not be seduced by lists of reasons why the effort will not succeed. Do not be tempted to reduce your vision or compromise your aspirations. Do not lose heart or joy or confidence.

If you do not have confidence, are not joyful, how can you expect donors to have confidence or to invest willingly?

Begin to look at the many obstacles, expressions of doubt, clever reasons why what you are about is "too grandiose," "too optimistic," "too foolhardy," or "unlikely if not impossible to achieve" as signs that you are on to something of consequence. Instead of being deflated and worried and dismayed by these assaults, look at them as clarion signs of progress, of rattling the cages, of imminent change. Banish cynicism.

My favorite definition of a cynic is this: a cynic is one who has given up but not yet shut up. Commit that to memory along with the maxim: the person who says it cannot be done should not interrupt the woman doing it!

On Overcoming Negative People

I am not sure I have ever spoken on the subject of fundraising and philanthropy when there hasn't been a question from a participant about how to handle and militate against the negativity of a key member of the board or staff. There are no perfect ways to respond to this, but several approaches in concert can make an impact.

First, limit contact with negative people whenever possible.

Second, resist the temptation to take personally another person's negativity, lack of confidence in the vision, rejection of proposed ideas, or long list of reasons why something will fail.

Third, try to learn, dispassionately, from the reasons they give for why something will fail, the better to anticipate and head off other people's resistance.

Fourth, learn to see obstacles, cynicism, and negativity as signs that you are on to something of consequence that is ushering in change, and see that the disquiet and resistance by some is simply an adverse reaction to change.

And finally, if the negative person or persons are in positions of influence, even leadership, and removing them from their positions of leadership is not an option, the best way to minimize their deleterious effect is to "dilute the pool." In other words, identify people who are more supportive and encouraging and who naturally command respect, and introduce them to the mix. Bring them onto the board, add them to the staff, or appoint them to a committee. Enlist them as a major donor or as an advisor, and allow their positive, confident, affirming, enthusiastic presence to trump the negativity expressed by others.

If you find a disproportionate amount of your time is spent dwelling on the difficult person or persons, try taking it to prayer. First, become mindful of where you are adding to the narrative and holding invented conversations in your mind. Resist the temptation to add to the narrative. It is neither fair nor faithful nor helpful. And it only serves to create even greater distance and disagreement between you and the difficult person. Then, try praying for the person with serious intention. Ask God to bless, console, affirm, and encourage the difficult person. In prayer let yourself be committed to the person's fulfillment. Try to see how God loves the person. Prayer changes the one praying, and soon you will become complicit in ensuring peace and fulfillment for the one who has caused anguish to your spirit. You will cultivate the capacity for mercy, and the triggers that otherwise cause you distress will soften and take on less importance.

> "Only in the world of mathematics do two negatives multiply into a positive."
>
> —Abby Morel

3

Before and After

Some of the obstacles to development have been identified. Helpful antidotes lie in spiritual maxims and guiding principles that are beneficial to full flourishing—both for a development program and for the ultimate objective of a successful development program: mission effectiveness.

Before highlighting these maxims and in order to draw illustratively from the primary example of our efforts to expand Catholic life on Yale's campus from September 16, 1997, to the dedication of the new center on December 1, 2006, it will be helpful to have a before-and-after snapshot contrast.

Before

In 1994 Fr. Bob was appointed the seventh Catholic chaplain at Yale. When he arrived on campus, he discovered 25 percent of the student population was Catholic, and he had inherited a host of administrative, financial, programmatic, and physical plant challenges to which he needed to attend with urgency. In the midst of those many challenges there was also something else: potential. Enormous potential.

And there were people to recognize that potential. A predominantly lay board, chaired by Judge Guido Calabresi, took the bold step to begin a comprehensive development effort, the first since the chaplaincy was created in 1922, and funds were raised to construct a Catholic chapel built in 1937. Ambitious goals were set. The campaign was program driven, grounded in mission, executed as a form of ministry, imbued with spirituality, with a loyalty to an urgent mission: help form young adult Catholics in a mature, adult faith, cognitively and affectively, that their faith might inspire, sustain, motivate, and inform all that they do as leaders on campus and far beyond its boundaries.

With Peter Alegi as chair of the building committee, John Wilkinson as owner's representative, Fay Vincent as chair of the development committee, a committed pastoral team, encouragement from the university and the archdiocese and alumni and many others committed to the vision, we were well blessed.

But it is important for anyone reading this to understand that we were not starting from scratch. It was far worse than that. There was financial debt on the books, a crumbling physical plant that was the consequence of years of deferred maintenance, meager student and faculty participation, sparsely attended Masses, one annual lecture, a shrinking operating budget, a growing operating deficit, a reduced and skeletal staff, and the elimination of 80 percent of the chaplaincy's database necessitating an outreach and apology as part of the communications strategy.

There was also the challenge that until recently both the number and percentage of Catholics attending Yale were small. This meant that there were few Catholic alumni and even fewer Catholic alumni capable of making a significant financial investment in the development effort. Compounding these conditions, I had been clear with Fr. Bob and Judge Calabresi before accepting the position, that a further sign of my weak candidacy for the role was the fact that I could not trespass on any of my relationships with the Catholic foundation community. I would have to be very attentive to full disclosure. I could ensure that the members of the foundations, my colleagues in philanthropy, were kept duly informed about the expanding ministry on Yale's campus, but I would not ask them for grant support.

What is important is that no matter how dire the situation appears there is always reason for hope if your mission is important and sound. In fact, the more dire the circumstances when you start, the greater a positive impact one can begin to have immediately. And with success comes momentum. The first step in the right direction encourages the second step. And as the president of our board, Judge Guido Calabresi, often remarked to us, "Nothing succeeds like success."

After

At the end of the campaign, we had raised fifteen times the original dollar goal and engaged students, faculty, alumni, parents, and prominent Catholic luminaries in the programmatic ministry. We had eliminated all debt, raised $25 million to construct a new center and renovate the chapel and chaplain's residence. We had expanded the operating budget by a factor of five and secured a $50 million endowment rivaling that of most small colleges. Fourteen new programmatic initiatives were introduced, including three endowed daylong fellowships in faith and science, religion and law, and faith and culture. We added a third Sunday liturgy at 10:00 p.m. to accommodate the growth in Mass attendance of young adults, who, we were always fond of pointing out, were there of their own volition, absent any parental pressure to attend.

We elevated the visibility of the ministry and inspired other Catholic campus ministries. Contemporary best board governance practices were adopted. We rebuilt and expanded the database and reclaimed lost contacts. The staff was expanded from five to seventeen. We entered into a partnership with Yale University Investments Office, led by David Swensen, in order that the Saint Thomas More endowment could be managed within the larger Yale investments portfolio, allowing us access to best in breed investment management and access to investment opportunities that would have otherwise been unavailable to us for lack of sufficient funds.

We built a 30,000-square-foot Cesar Pelli–designed Catholic student center, debt-free, on property leased from Yale to the Catholic community for ninety-nine years for one payment of twenty dollars. We created a national young adult leadership formation program for Catholic students at Yale and on campuses across the country.

But most of all we elicited and responded to the students' vitality, hope, joy, young adult energy, and passion while providing them formation in adult mature faith lives, cognitively and affectively.

How did this transformation happen? So much of the impetus for writing this book is a desire to answer that question.

Each ensuing chapter focuses on particular aspects of development we found to be essential to our success and happened to correlate beautifully with spiritual maxims we tried to incorporate into our daily lives. For so long the challenge has been that people of interior spirituality, people who daily cultivate faith and grow in self-awareness and compassion, have assumed that these very attributes have no bearing on the efficacy of fundraising. The presumption is that to be a good fundraiser one must have aptitude that is very different from that which we associate with formation for religious life and skills we expect to be irrelevant or even contrary to spiritual maturation. No wonder the resistance and discomfort. Imagine how differently you might approach the task of raising money if you were convinced that the core attributes you needed to be successful were the very attributes that led to your discernment to lead a life of service, or to become a priest or minister, or to work in the nonprofit sector in the first place. And what if I told you that these attributes would be called forth, tested, strengthened, and honed in ways beyond your wildest imagination in service to development? That at the end of the story, you would be far more the person you were meant to be, yearned to be, and the mission of your organization would be radically expanded, elevated to a far wider audience and that you would have been instrumental in raising all the money needed?

The tenth verse of the tenth chapter of the Gospel according to John is "Jesus said, 'I came that they might have life, and have it more abundantly.'" In an elegant foreshadowing of all that would be accomplished on Yale's campus, Fr. Bob and I discovered early in our work together that we each had this as our favorite verse from Scripture. It was the first of many moments when it was clear we shared a spirituality that would radically influence our service to expand Catholic life at Yale. We let John 10:10 inform our work together. We took it to prayer and held to the conviction that we were instruments of all that God intended, that students not even yet born would one day experience this promise of a more abundant life by being welcomed into Catholic life at Yale, exposed to the rich tradition of our faith, given opportunities to grow intellectually and affectively in faith, and be invited into a life of discipleship, of service, and of justice.

The turning point came when we directly confronted our biases and misperceptions and the false premise about fundraising from which we had been operating. It did not happen immediately but gradually, through prayer, reflection, and experience. We came to appreciate that development is ministry, that donors are not objects but subjects. We realized that money matters intimately to people and that this can be an invitation to sacred and meaningful conversations. We learned to equate the activity of development with sharing good news and saw how clearly the world yearns for good news. We became aware that among the positive consequences of successful fundraising for faith-based ministries are engagement and evangelization. We witnessed how effectively money follows mission and that fundraising allows for conversion of mind and heart, collaboration in a compelling mission, rooted in faith, benefiting others. In short: philanthropy and fundraising can be profound expressions of what is most deeply meaningful in life. And we had front-row seats.

4

Worthy of Generosity

The Starting Point Is Gratitude

I had the great privilege of knowing Henri Nouwen.

We first met in 1995 when he returned to Yale Divinity School to participate in a series of wonderful events in conjunction with the Special Olympics, led so capably by our inspiring friend Tim Shriver. Henri had famously taught at Yale many years ago but had now, by his own admission, found his true home. He lived with mentally and physically disabled adults in a community called L'Arche, founded by Jean Vanier in Toronto. Henri Nouwen had joined Yale's faculty on the same day as another illustrious faculty member, Sr. Margaret Farley, RSM, and they had remained friends ever since. At Tim Shriver's request, Margaret had extended an invitation to Henri to speak at Yale Divinity School with Adam, one of his L'Arche community members, and separately to have dinner and an informal discussion with members of the Catholic community at the Divinity School.

I was pregnant with my first child, due any moment, and I worried labor might prevent me from attending and hearing Fr. Nouwen's reflections.

The baby cooperated, and I learned something that has remained with me ever since and set the foundation for all I would come to learn about philanthropy and fundraising. It is also perhaps the greatest spiritual lesson of our lives.

Henri Nouwen said, "The central truth of your life—of all of our lives—is to know, to know truly and completely, that God loves you just for being you." He went on to explain that we spend all of our adult lives doubting this, talking ourselves out of this, refusing to believe it, arguing against it. But every once in a while we experience the profound conviction of God's radical unalterable love for us. And that is a powerful, transformative moment of grace.

> "From beginning to end, fundraising as ministry is grounded in prayer and undertaken in gratitude."
>
> —Henri Nouwen

As I reflected on this, I realized how important his insight is. If you have experienced what Henri is speaking about, you know a profound gratitude that permeates your whole being. It is like being wildly, fully in love with someone, and in the midst of that undeniable yearning suddenly realizing that he or she is in love with you, too. That moment of requited love is a joy that exudes gratitude. When you realize how much God loves you, you want to love God back. And the desire to express that gratitude knows no end. But how do you love God back?

When our son Christopher was a little boy, he received what his heart desired most on Christmas day from Santa: a small plastic saxophone. So full was his joy, so immense was his gratitude that he turned to the bevy of aunts and uncles, parents and grandparents assembled by the tree and pointing to his uncle Rich said, "Pretend you're Santa Claus!" And then addressing Uncle Rich said, "Thank you, Santa Claus! Thank you! Thank you for my saxophone!" And he rushed forward to wrap his small arms around his uncle in total abandon.

To be sure, Christopher believed in Santa, but he needed Santa to be incarnate, physically present, in order to express more tangibly his gratitude.

This is what we experience as adults, too, when we know of God's love: the extraordinary desire to love God back, to say thank you, to express how much the gift of God's love matters.

Henri went on to say that the way to love God back, the way to express gratitude to God for the blessings of God's love, is to love all that God has created and therefore also loves: creation, each other, life. And you love what God has created by being fruitful with your own life.

I was riveted to Henri's insight and his conviction. I rose from my chair, struggling with my enormous pregnant body and sheepishly offered, "I have a sense of what 'be fruitful and multiply' entails, but what do you mean by being more broadly fruitful with one's life? What does that concretely look like?"

If you knew Henri, you can easily picture his reaction. He could laugh with his whole being, giving in to joy and delight, a hallmark of the spiritual life. When he recovered, he elaborated upon what it means to be fruitful, giving example after example of the pattern. Being fruitful means recognizing that all that has been given to us is an expression of God's love for us. Everything comes from God. We begin with gratitude for such blessings, and we desire to love God back. We love God back by being fruitful with our lives, which is to take all that has been given to us and to place it at the service of others, of creation, of life itself. It is to be a beneficial presence. It is to contribute and bless, rather than to take or condemn. It is to demonstrate our love for God by loving all that God loves and attending to whom and what God loves by giving our whole selves in service. It was the clearest illustration of stewardship I had ever been given.

Much has been written about the importance of gratitude in fundraising: showing appreciation to donors, thanking donors, acknowledging donors' generosity. All of this is most certainly important, but Henri's insight goes deeper and suggests that there is a more important starting point for gratitude. We have often been too limited in our appreciation of this, relegating it only to discussions of money and material generosity. To be sure donors are often motivated to give generously, to invest in programs and activities that in turn bless the lives of others out of a stance of gratitude for the good fortune and blessings in their own lives. But we do a disservice to the fundamental spiritual insight here if we only think about this in the context of financial gifts, giving money out of gratitude, receiving money in gratitude, and expressing thanks to donors for giving money. Money is valuable but is not the only blessing we have at our disposal. We also have time, presence, intellectual expertise, experience, talent, wisdom, compassion, mercy, stamina, joy, encouragement, and faith to name a few of the blessings we are also called to recognize, be grateful for, and offer.

On Counting Miracles

I was seven months pregnant with our second child when I began my first day as director of development for Saint Thomas More Catholic Chapel and Center at Yale on September 16, 1997.

Our daughter was due on Thanksgiving, which I thought was perfectly appropriate. I literally could not wait for her to be born. But wait I did; Sophie was two weeks late, consequently the longest part of my pregnancy fell to Advent. Waiting in joyful expectation took on profoundly tangible meaning. Every day I expected this miracle of new life. I yearned for her arrival on the scene. Patience was exacting.

One of the miracles of giving birth is the effect of a baby on our perception of time. Time slows to its most manageable capacity. Parents see all of life through the eyes of their child, with rapt wonder. Not since I was a child myself do I remember paying such intimate, close attention to the permeations of seasons.

> "Miracles happen everyday, change your perception of what a miracle is and you'll see them all around you."
>
> —Jon Bon Jovi

Sophie came home to a warm and welcoming house with a Christmas tree already decorated. Every evening of her first few weeks of life, she and I would wake in the darkest hour of the darkest days of the calendar, find our way into our living room by the beautifully lit tree, and I would nurse her and read to her and tell her how unconditionally loved she is. We spent hours alone together each night marveling at the magical quality of light cast off by hundreds of tiny white bulbs. I explained the significance and history of each unique and precious ornament, gifts especially of her great-grandmother and others eager to meet and welcome her to our wide, extended family.

Each Christmas she is reminded of how we spent her early days of life, and each Christmas we engage in our tradition of counting Christmas miracles. Our favorite year, we counted twenty-six Christmas miracles, ranging from the perfect parking spot in a last mad dash of preparations, to the exhilarating surprise visit of my brother, Peter, and sister-in-law, Theresa, on a snowy Christmas morning, to the discovery of a bird's nest deep within our Christmas tree.

We wait for the birth of Christ and the reign of God, impeccable responses to our deepest desires: for intimacy, love, reconciliation, meaning, and an end to violence, poverty, illness, and death. We are hard-wired for God, and yearning for God is both joyful and excruciating.

Take time to count miracles with someone you cherish. You will be surprised by how many you find as you allow time to slow down, allow yourself to be present to grace, and marvel at God's presence in our human lives, reminding us always of what full, beautiful, transcendent life is yet to come.

Stewardship of Potential

My cousins and I grew up with this curious word "stewardship." We understood that we were expected to be stewards of the Raskob Foundation's resources. One definition of stewardship is the proper care of all that has been entrusted to one. This is hard enough to achieve, but for a person of faith, stewardship requires more. For a person of faith, stewardship is both the proper care of all that has been entrusted to one *and* the recognition of and response to the potential at hand.

Tom Locke, a wonderful friend and exemplary leader of Texas Methodist Foundation in Austin, engaged his board and staff in a dynamic, faith-filled, reflective visioning process that resulted in a subtle but meaningful shift in the strategic focus of their philanthropic service to Methodist congregations, encapsulated in their new tagline, "Stewarding Potential." In their 2013 annual report is written "Stewarding potential is about abundance, not scarcity. It points us toward a God whose desire and potential for us is 'abundant life,'

life that is fulfilled by accomplishing God-appointed missions, not self-appointed preferences, life that is filled with meaning, gratitude, and generosity."

When he told me about the process of reflection and the promising, energizing outcome, I was reminded of Ghandi's insight, "The difference between what we do and what we are capable of doing would suffice to solve most of the world's problems."

What does it mean to recognize and attend to potential? Most of us have complicated, full lives with multiple responsibilities. We would certainly be doing well simply to care adequately for that which has been entrusted to us. When we go beyond what has been entrusted to us and notice potential, how do we respond? Often we respond with a disclaimer, "I have enough responsibility to manage right now." "I can't take on one more thing." "Sure it has potential, but the amount of work required to realize that potential comes at too great a cost." "It might have potential, but it is a big risk that it would fail." "That really should be somebody else's job." And so on.

Being responsible for the financial health or expansion of a non-profit or ministry affords a wonderful opportunity to reflect on potential. The starting goal is to help the ministry be worthy of generosity. To commit to being worthy of generosity means to care for every aspect of the ministry to ensure high levels of excellence. For authenticity's sake and for maximum effect, this must be as broadly comprehensive as possible. It is not enough to have a charismatic, trustworthy leader and a compelling mission, although these are

> "I wondered why somebody didn't do something. Then I realized, I am somebody."
>
> —unknown

sacrosanct essentials. It is also necessary to ensure that every component that affects the nonprofit's mission is of the highest quality. This extends to the management of people, facilities, and finances, the mechanisms and modes of communications, the use of technology, and strategic planning. Furthermore it is important to ensure that one's intentional implementation of best managerial practices is current and effective. And even when all of this is achieved, there is still the matter of being a good steward of the potential, the opportunities, at hand.

My inspiring, dear friend, Gerry Roche, senior chair of Heidrick & Struggles for many years, voted "headhunter of the century" by his peers in the executive recruiting industry, once told me that among the saddest things in his entire life is bearing witness to unfulfilled potential. It was his life's work to identify talent and match competencies with opportunities. What he anguished over was recognizing the potential in someone and seeing circumstance or choices preventing them from fulfilling that potential.

I often wonder if God feels similarly. Having endowed humankind with intelligence, free will, and unlimited global potential—including the abilities to be merciful, forgiving, and loving—does God anguish over our individual and collective failure to recognize it, let alone act on it?

Winning the Lottery

My generous-hearted sister-in-law, Terri Cappello, began a recent conversation this way:

"Every day I pass an enormous billboard on my way to work that indicates the current tally of total winnings available, and I imagine what I would do if I won the lottery."

Being the compassionate and thoughtful woman she is, her plans included using the money to help other people pursue and live their dreams.

I have had this conversation with friends and strangers alike over many years and am always struck by the inherent generosity most people's plans reveal. There is, for example, almost always the expressed intention of giving away some portion to charity. Often people name others they would specifically like to help: a child, a parent, a sibling, a friend. And there is frequently a desire to use the lottery to fulfill a lifelong personal dream, doing that which one was seemingly born to do. These conversations always make me wish everyone could win the lottery, for how much more generous, authentically experienced, and other-centered life would be.

But for the first time, in conversation with my sister-in-law, I became acutely aware of an undeniable fact: we have already won the lottery.

"Winning the lottery" implies a random, undeserved gift of good fortune awarded by chance. Hasn't each of us already won? Perhaps we have won the lottery with our health or with loving relationships with our parents or children or siblings. Maybe we have won the lottery with our intellectual or creative aptitude, the opportunity for meaningful work, the chance to be paid for a job we adore, talents we get to employ for the common good, a superb sense of style, charisma, charm, or an excellent sense of humor. Perhaps we won the lottery with a marriage or life partnership of profound mutual love, support, and respect. Maybe we won the lottery with physical safety, emotional security, shelter, enough food for ourselves and our families. Perhaps we won the lottery by being able to attend wonderful schools, with inspiring teachers, or by having the ability to provide that opportunity for our children. Others of us may have won the lottery with the gift of faith, an abiding trust in Providence, an irrepressible hope, or a profound awareness of the beauty of creation and the dignity of humankind.

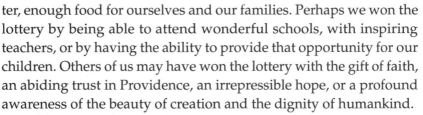

"If we had no hope—for a cure, for winning the lottery, for falling in love, for the end of war, for being free of abuse, or for having food, warmth, clothing, and shelter—we would have no reason to go on. What you hope for doesn't matter, but rather the essence of hope itself."

—Bernie Siegel

How many lotteries in life has each of us already won?

So here is the question, the responsibility, the unavoidable point: What are we actually doing with all that we have won?

Do we persist in daring to complain of scarcity?

Do we share our abundance with others?

Do we give some portion to charity?

Do we live with awareness and gratitude?

Do we live in an other-centered way, attending to the needs of humankind?

Do we live the life we were meant to live, with integrity and authenticity and joy?

That very excitement and energetic outpouring of creative ideas, especially concerning helping others "if I won the lottery" is accessible to every one of us right now. We have the desire, and we have the plan. Only we've already won.

Time to put the plan in motion. That is being fruitful with one's life. That is stewardship.

The Leadership Virtue of Prescience and Tenacity

I never knew my great-grandfather; he died before I was born. But several stories are legendary in the family lore.

One of them concerns the days following Governor Al Smith's failed bid to be the president of the United States of America. John Raskob was the chair of the Democratic National Party when Al Smith was running for president—the first Catholic to do so. After the election, legend has it that Al was lamenting his fate in the men's room of the Waldorf Astoria in New York City. He was upset that his career seemed effectively over. He could not go back to being governor of New York. He was despondent.

At this precise moment, dramatically from the shadows of the men's room, came the voice of John Raskob: "Do not despair, my friend. I have a new idea. I will finance, and we will build the world's tallest building, and you will be the president of that corporation."

A press conference was called to announce what would become the creation of the Empire State Building. Only, shortly afterward, the market crashed. It was 1929. No one expected John Raskob to keep his plans, but it was a matter of integrity and prescience to him. The building project continued—but now thousands of men were employed to give as many people work as possible. Multiple records were broken as the building rose.

> "When we plant a tree, we don't plant it for ourselves but for our children."
>
> —The Reverend Mae "Mother" Wyatt

Today it is one of the most iconic buildings in the world. But here is the little-known fact: it took forty years before the building reached full occupancy. Most people scoffed at the folly of his idea and determination. But John Raskob was a remarkable leader of profound vision. He was prescient and knew that he did not need to live to see the results of his vision and hard work for it to have value for others.

It has been said that the greater the leader, the farther out extends the leader's vision. While many of us are looking toward the end of the week in anticipation of Friday, a great leader is looking out forty or fifty years to anticipate a future. A necessary corollary is courage and tenacity, the ability to stick to one's vision and conviction when everything else is conspiring to dissuade you of that vision.

I have marveled my whole life at the tenacity of visionaries who work toward a more just and charitable world. It is activity not for the faint of heart. To be committed is to be committed for the long haul. My best friend quips that "if you need to see the immediate results of your work, paint houses."

Imagine all that can be brought to fruition by leaders who possess this particular constellation of qualities: prescience, courage, tenacity, and a radical commitment to making this a better, more just, and joyous world.

The Divine Tenacity of Love

This story takes place in a setting of abject poverty. Mother Teresa is caring for the dying in Calcutta, and there is one man who resents her care, rejects her attendant ablutions, spits in her face when she tries to administer medicine and comfort. This contentious relationship carries on for days, as the man, with no family or friends, lies dying. And still Mother Teresa comes to him, washes him, feeds him, extends her compassion. He argues with her, tells her he does not believe in God, he does not believe in human kindness. He wants to be left alone to die alone. He is angry, bitter, demoralized, radically ungrateful. And still she comes to him that he might have dignity in his final days. She cleans his own filth, dresses him in fresh clothes, spoons broth into his mouth. Weakly he tries to swat her hands away, admonishes her for her care. Until, frightened, knowing these are the final hours of his life, he leans into her arms as she holds him, looks up at her, and begs of her, "Please. Is your God like you?"

> "I have found the paradox, that if you love until it hurts, there can be no more hurt, only more love."
>
> —Mother Teresa

Money Follows Mission

Often boards and nonprofit leaders will reject an idea for growth or a new program that will help advance the mission with the declaration that "we don't have the money" or "it isn't in the budget." There is often an insistence on raising money first and then advancing the mission of the organization.

While a case can be made for why this approach is fiscally responsible, it all too often is used as an excuse for inertia, maintenance, avoiding innovation, stagnant thinking, and continued mediocrity. Mission must always come first, new possibilities recognized, and opportunities considered, particularly if one desires to be worthy of generosity. It is far more important to ensure the mission of a nonprofit is being advanced in an effective, relevant, and life-giving way than it is to ensure that revenue is increasing.

Obviously the two are linked, and without revenue one's ability to introduce a new program, staff member, partnership, or innovation might be compromised. The goal is to achieve both: an expansion of mission through new and novel programs that serve to bring potential to fruition *and* financial health to allow for such expansion. The most successful, dynamic, well-funded nonprofits always begin by living out of mission, so that rather than just talk about their mission, they can show donors how they are acting on that mission. There is a far greater integrity and far more compelling example to point to when done in this order. Given the choice of which to act on first, choose mission every single time. Commit to mission, ensure that everything is being done to be worthy of generosity, recognize and act on the potential at hand, bring energy and passion, joy and innovation to the equation, and see how quickly money follows mission.

Shortly after Fr. Bob had been appointed Catholic chaplain at Yale, a trustee called him on the phone to welcome him to his new role. And much to Fr. Bob's astonishment said, "Take my advice Father. Shutter the Chapel for two years, get out on the road and raise money, and then come back and reopen." It had been a difficult decision for Fr. Bob to leave parish ministry, which he loved, to come to campus ministry, which was new. But one thing was certain. He did not make that decision and transition only to preside over the temporary closing of Catholic campus ministry at Yale in order to raise money. Politely he expressed this to the trustee, but from that point forward he paid attention to just how serious the financial challenge before him was.

The trustee was not being punitive. He was simply drawing attention to the fiscal realities of the situation at hand. For several years Yale's Catholic campus ministry had been operating at a deficit. Each year the board reduced the operating budget by reducing staff and programming, and yet each year the deficit grew. In fact, so serious was the fiscal distress that two decisions were made by the board that had unintended deleterious consequences when it came time for the capital campaign to begin.

The first was that to cover the operating deficit, money was borrowed from Saint Thomas More Chapel's small endowment, which was indicated each year in the audit. Inspiring donor generosity and confidence would require resolving the debt and having a clean audit. Second, 80 percent of the mailing list was permanently deleted on the grounds that it was profligate to continue to pay for postage to send an annual dunning letter to alumni who had not contributed in ten or more years.

This was the landscape we inherited when we announced the start of the capital campaign. A skeletal staff, greatly reduced programming,

a crumbling facility desperately in need of basic capital improve-
ments, debt on the books, a tiny operating budget, understandably
high fiscal anxiety on the part of the trustees who were the fiduciary
agents of the ministry, and a reduction of at least 80 percent of the
Yale Catholic alumni constituency who consequently had not received
any communication from or about the Chapel in years. The board
was hardly to be blamed for its caution about expanding the program
and living out of mission given the harsh fiscal realities at hand.

And yet, given the choice to begin with mission and program or
to begin with raising money and resolving the debt, there was no
question what Fr. Bob and I would choose. There was a focus to our
work, to our vocation, to our aspiration, and to our vision. We had
to start with the mission, find opportunities to advance that mission,
and be far better stewards of the resources at our disposal. We needed
to trust that as we offered students credible and compelling opportunities to cultivate a mature adult life of faith and introduced new
and novel programming, the direction would change. The goal was
to ensure that everything that was offered to students, from liturgy
to intellectual programming to social justice opportunities, was done
at a very high level of excellence. With innovative, welcoming, high-
quality programs, there would be an increase in student participation.
With an increase in student participation, the visibility of our expanding ministry would be strengthened. By reversing the direction of
our ministry from diminishment to growth, money would follow.

Let me be clear, this was an arduous, demanding task, requiring
our complete commitment. An image has remained with me since
those very early days of the campaign. It is the image of an aircraft
carrier, a ship so massive it is capable of carrying, deploying, and
recovering aircraft at sea. Big enough for planes to land on its floating
runway! Imagine the sheer weight and mass of such a ship. Now
imagine that it is progressing in a certain direction that is exactly the
opposite direction from where you would like the ship to be going.
What would it take to turn that ship around? A lot!

If you don't change course, you will end up where you are heading. It takes time and energy to reverse course. The arc of travel alone
required to completely reverse direction renders you helpless to the
perception that no movement or progress is being made. Undoing
past mistakes, making amends for past transgressions, doing "dam-
age control," eliminating debt, undoing bad habits, charting a new

course, and inculcating good habits and managerial disciplines—all take time and perseverance. It can be painstaking to endure, but it is essential. But when you are at last headed in the right direction, the progress forward is swift, almost effortless.

The very first task was to take a fresh look at our mission, a practice that is healthy and important for board and staff members of every nonprofit on an ongoing basis. This is the first step of a strategic plan. We asked ourselves: What is our mission? Is it relevant? Does it respond to an unmet need? Is it urgent? Is it clear? Is it compelling? If we ceased to exist, would it matter? This exercise allowed Fr. Bob and me to return to our original discernment prior to assuming our respective roles on behalf of Catholic life at Yale. Important to both of us was our commitment to attend to the 25 percent of the Yale student body

> "Every time we approach people for money, we must be sure that we are inviting them into this vision of fruitfulness and into a vision that is fruitful."
>
> —Henri Nouwen

that identified as Catholic to ensure that everything possible would be done to help them grow in a mature, adult faith, cognitively and affectively. This was not solely so that the students would develop spiritually and interiorly as they advanced intellectually, physically, and socially. The mission was important because the ages of eighteen to twenty-five represent a crucially formative period of life, and if students did not have the opportunity to cultivate an adult mature faith during these years, they might likely never prioritize it.

Furthermore, we knew that they had extraordinary gifts and by virtue of admission to Yale, nearly unlimited future opportunities for leadership and influence. We wanted to equip them to be inspired, informed, nurtured, consoled, and sustained by their faith in their formative years of study and to have recourse to it as they assumed positions of leadership and influence across every conceivable sector and industry. Furthermore, we did not want the church to miss out—now or years from now—on this talented pool of well-educated, energetic, caring, and capable young adults.

All of that, and we were committed to raising the bar of Catholic campus ministry nationally through the example we were setting at Yale.

Shortly after I found myself accepting the invitation to work on behalf of Saint Thomas More Chapel, by chance I was seated next to Bishop Peter Rosazza on a propeller plane from Tweed New Haven Airport to Washington National. Bishop Peter was an auxiliary bishop of the Archdiocese of Hartford and had recently learned from Fr. Bob that I had accepted the position. Bishop Peter and I had known each other for many years through involvement with the Raskob Foundation, and we shared a love of young adult ministry and social justice. It was Bishop Peter who nominated me to serve on the Catholic Campaign for Human Development board, the United States Conference of Catholic Bishops' effort to reduce poverty and injustice in America. I served for five terms, and in the course of those fifteen years developed wonderful relationships with the bishops with whom I shared a commitment to advancing Catholic social justice tradition in the United States.

It was a very long flight to Washington. Bishop Peter simply could not understand how I could have said "yes to Yale" that already had so many resources. He argued that my energy would be better served working on behalf of one of the many social justice and poverty relief apostolates about which he and I cared so deeply.

I took a deep breath and pondered his question, somewhat taken aback by the passion of his conviction. And then I remembered that he himself had matriculated at Dartmouth. And so I explained that I had prayed long and hard about this for five days, that I didn't want to have anything to do with it when I was first approached, that I hated the idea of raising money, that I had been warned about the fiscal distress of the chaplaincy many years earlier, that I had resisted even then my normal inclination to offer to help with advice on approaching some foundations that might be supportive of campus ministry. It was nearly preposterous to find myself agreeing to the role. And then I explained to my friend, Bishop Peter, that we didn't make the rules of the world, but like it or not, the students who attended and graduated from Yale would go on to influential leadership positions. They would be heads of state, executives of international corporations, influential writers, thought leaders, activists, and artists. Didn't he think it was important that they be fully formed in an adult, mature faith that can inspire their leadership, so that one day the decisions they make that could have an impact on hundreds of thousands of other people would be informed by Catholic social justice teaching, for example?

Again and again, we found it essential to be radically committed to our mission and to a vision of where we were heading. We had to be clear about our mission and be able to articulate it at a moment's notice. We lived vocationally. Every waking thought was about how to advance the mission in a credible, effective, faith-filled way. We lived and breathed mission. Even to this day, nearly eight years since my formal role at Yale came to an end, I can launch right into an impassioned declaration of the importance of Catholic campus ministry at Yale.

Once we were clear about and committed to our mission, attentive to the potential we wanted to bring to fruition, and aspirational and visionary about our future, we needed to act on it.

But there was still the matter of having no money in the budget, no authorization from the board to spend money we did not have, and the board's expectation that we would be increasing financial health, not adding to the debt by investing in new programming no matter how visionary and compelling such programs might be.

An important lesson was born by this dilemma: never, ever give up. If your intentions are sound, if the mission is compelling, if it is the right thing to do, find a way to make it happen.

So we began to look for resources. And in the process discovered that we had one tremendously underutilized resource, perhaps the greatest resource at our disposal, and we had failed to recognize it as such. It was the constellation of some eighty-eight Catholic faculty members at Yale across every department and discipline.

Yale's faculty are famous in their fields and are routinely invited to give lectures all across the globe. Not only were these men and women local, requiring no investment of travel or accommodations, by not involving them personally and meaningfully in our mission we were failing to attend to part of our core constituency. At its most rudimentary our mission was to provide Catholic ministry to Yale students, faculty, and staff.

We set about identifying as comprehensively as possible the members of Yale's faculty who were Catholic. And then we invited each faculty member to speak to the students after the 5:00 p.m. Mass on Sunday every month. We encouraged them not to speak about their scholarship and research but rather to speak about their personal lives of faith. Students knew these brilliant professors as intellectual heroes and heroines but didn't often think about them as religious or spiritual. It was vital that we demonstrated at every opportunity that being smart and Catholic was not an oxymoron; a core component of our ministry was to help students develop a vocabulary for speaking about their faith and to access and appreciate the rich tradition of Catholic intellectual life.

And thus was born the first of many new initiatives we introduced as part of our expansion. Entitled "Life as a Scholar and a Believer," students were invited to the Chapel Hall (in the basement) for a simple meal and were treated each month to the uniquely personal stories of faculty. It is the only time we ever saw Yale faculty nervous. They were nervous because so few of us are ever invited to speak about something so intimate as our personal lives of faith. Each story was deeply compelling. Members of the faculty spoke about how their faith had informed their vocation to academic life and teaching, how their faith had consoled them in times of deep personal loss, how their faith expanded their sense of wonder, meaning, transcendence. Students sat in rapt attention as Guido Calabresi, Teresa Berger, Lamin Sanneh, Cynthia Russett, Thomas Duffy, Patricia Ryan-Krause, and Leo Hickey—to name but a few—candidly revealed an intimate piece of their faith lives.

And the questions that followed were wonderful. Lamin Sanneh spoke about being raised Muslim in Africa, converting to Christianity, and then becoming Catholic during the Easter Vigil at Saint Thomas More at Yale with Cardinal Avery Dulles as his sponsor. A student asked him, "Was there anything in Islam that you valued that you don't find in Christianity that you miss?" Professor Sanneh replied, "Yes, reverence for the name of God." This provided weeks of discussion for students about where reverence for God is in their own spirituality.

And what was the outcome of the introduction of this new initiative? The members of the Yale faculty we had identified as Catholic were formally invited to participate in the mission of the campus ministry, were welcomed and reminded that even if they belonged to a Catholic parish in the suburbs of New Haven, this was always properly their spiritual home, too, and they and their families were always welcome. Students who had never before attended an event or even a Mass at Saint Thomas More Chapel began to attend regularly, drawn to the personal and often riveting life stories of their revered professors. Soon they were noticing and being attracted to the quality of everything else they were exposed to through campus ministry. The initiative allowed us to promote Saint Thomas More Chapel and our ministries. The visibility of the Chapel and attendant ministries was elevated. Reporters wrote stories about the initiative. And when Fr. Bob and I traveled to meet Yale Catholic alumni to talk about the expansion of Catholic life on campus, our development goals and plans, and how we were advancing our mission, this was a perfect example of relevant, innovative, thoughtful programming we could showcase. Alumni loved it. And they began to respond with increased donations for "general operating support," a prelude to a more significant investment in the building fund. By every measure it was an enormous success, beneficial to multiple constituencies and helpful to meet many objectives in our zeal to be comprehensive and excellent. Everyone benefited. The second lesson: When it is a win-win-win scenario, when everyone benefits, grace is operative.

And all of this for the price of a spaghetti dinner once a month.

Often there are resources at hand that have never been recognized or utilized. Start by identifying those resources, and put them to excellent use.

6

Habits of Inner Life for Outward Service

I had the great good fortune to spend an evening in Manhattan with three of the world's most insightful spiritual thought leaders of our time—four if you count Stephen Colbert.

Our evening began on the set of the *Colbert Report*, witness to an uproarious live filming, and concluded with dinner in a tiny, joyfully boisterous trattoria on the west side. Conversation and laughter were unfettered; our shared penchant for friendship, conviviality, and humor over martinis and pasta was evident.

I could not resist a personal question, given my incongruous presence in the company of spiritual heroes whose writings, reflections, and homilies have inspired hundreds of thousands of people over four decades and a globe. I was conscious that this privileged time together in their company was soon coming to a close. I risked the question:

"What is the single most valuable insight, attribute, or discipline you ascribe to personally—and advise others to cultivate—in order to live a life of fulfillment, peace, and joy?" In short, I was hoping to discover what the one sacrosanct spiritual virtue was for each of them, crystalized to its simplest.

Without hesitation they replied in quiet, succinct, rapid succession. "Be forgiving," said the first. "Be kind," stated the second. "Be grateful," concluded the third.

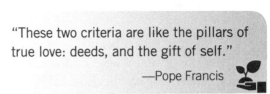

"These two criteria are like the pillars of true love: deeds, and the gift of self."

—Pope Francis

Forgiveness, kindness, and gratitude. Simple precepts, shared with humility and conviction, offered as grace.

We would do well to resolve to be more forgiving of each other and ourselves, to be kinder to all we encounter, and to live with intentional gratitude.

Personal Moral Heroes and Heroines

We all have personal moral heroes and heroines. Pay attention to those you have in your own life. They are quietly inspiring, rarely famous, and almost never aware that they would be seen as heroic. Identify the qualities you most identify with them, and learn to emulate those qualities.

My grandfather, Charles Apel Robinson, was buried on his ninety-second birthday. The cause of death was simply that he had come to the end of a long and wondrous life, a life we irrationally presumed might be immortal.

Decades ahead of his time, Charlie was a champion of racial, economic, and environmental justice. The moral code informing his life made obvious that every person counted, that the whole world was interconnected, and that we were mandated to care for one other, across religious, national, and ethnic boundaries. He promoted peace and reconciliation. He loved the earth, the land, its people, and life itself.

Most of all he loved his wife, Josephine, to whom, at the precise moment of her birth on July 4 he introduced himself, a precocious ten-year-old setting off a phalanx of fireworks beneath her first window. For the next eighty-two years they were coconspirators in grace and mercy, justice and hospitality. Together they had fourteen children, seven of whom were adopted. Countless others, many exchange students from across the globe, were warmly enveloped into their family and home.

His life is worthy of volumes, but one memory is particularly illustrative.

Picture this: a beautiful, warm, sunny day in June. Hundreds of people of many ages and nations are gathered at a teahouse and garden in the countryside. Life is bursting forth and joyful celebration is in the air. Martinis (gin, of course) are served, perfectly. Bagpipers parade the lawn. The banquet is bounteous. There are reservoirs of laughter and the curious joy unique to reunion. Stories—familiar, embellished, and new—are told, privately and communally. And there are many, many tears. This is Charlie's wake.

Hours pass. His body is laid out in an antechamber. Flowers, memorabilia, and framed photographs adorn the casket. We take turns saying our final good-byes, kneeling by his body, praying that he is already in God's full embrace, that he will be our intercessor, that he knows how much we love him and will miss him. We give thanks for his life, for his example, for calling us to be better people in service to a world in need.

> "Goodness is about character—integrity, honesty, kindness, generosity, moral courage, and the like. More than anything else, it is about how we treat other people."
>
> —Dennis Prager

One by one, in pairs, in small groups we exit the teahouse. The sun is setting; the wake has lasted all day. We are simultaneously depleted and replenished. No one wants to take final leave of this heartbreaking setting. We take our time, cross the long swath of freshly mown grass, and stop to take a last look back to where our deeply loved father, grandfather, great-grandfather, colleague, neighbor, friend, and moral hero is in repose. We linger, mournfully, gratefully. Hundreds of people who loved Charlie are present, gathered in hushed tones at the edge of the garden, aching with unnamed longing, unwilling to part.

And then, as though rewarding us for our hesitation, the last mourner passes through the door. From this distance, my grandmother looks small, vulnerable, and regal all at once. We are silent in reverence and empathy. Two of her sons come to her side. Lovingly escorted, she makes her long journey across the wide expanse of lawn toward all we have to offer: our spontaneous, sustained applause that seems to never end.

The Intimate Connection of Prayer and Gratitude

Every other weekend for the entirety of my childhood we would drive from Washington, DC, to Hartefeld, the bucolic farm on which my paternal grandparents lived. We were never the only guests. My grandparents had an innate, defining quality of hospitality that informed their open invitation to countless foreign exchange students, extended relatives, college friends of their fourteen children, and generations of missionary priests and nuns working to alleviate human suffering and promote social justice all over the globe. Their spacious home, with ten bedrooms, was always full. A glance at the flagpole as one approached the house at the end of a long and winding driveway provided a clue to the nationalities of the guests expected on any given weekend.

One evening, late in June, daylight lingered long after a meal for twenty-five relatives and friends, a common scene at Hartefeld. Uncharacteristically, I excused myself from the table taking with me the scent of cigars and coffee, the echo of laughter and stories told and retold, the confidence of belonging to this boisterous, eccentric, loving family. I wanted to take a walk down the long expanse of lawn, around the small acre of quiet lake, and back up to the warm, well-lit, inviting house. By choice, I rarely was alone, much preferring to be in the company of my cousins, aunts, and uncles. I hated to be put to bed before the grown-ups. Even when I couldn't understand the conversations at hand, I wanted to stay and absorb the atmosphere, the cadence of discourse, the passionate debates, the enticing vocabulary, and the inevitable laughter. I was born an extrovert and reveled in the company of others. The more people at the party, the happier I was. And yet, on this occasion I left of my own accord, quietly and unobtrusively, to walk in solitude.

It is my first memory of prayer.

I was eight years old. Solitude seemed urgent and necessary for me to concentrate on what I was experiencing. As I walked toward and around the lake, I was bursting with energy, with an overwhelming sense of gratitude, with limitless love and appreciation for what I could not even name as blessing. I yearned to communicate what I felt, but my childhood vocabulary was inadequate to the task. I walked faster, with greater earnestness, desperate to name my joy, express my gratitude, account comprehensively for the abundance for which I was grateful:

"In prayer it is better to have a heart without words than words without a heart."

—John Bunyan

my family, the setting, the example of my grandparents' guests making this a better and more just world, my wonderful cousins, our laughter, post-prandial piano music and Cole Porter songs, fireflies, safety, love. I didn't know how to express it, and the frustration was nearly unbearable.

In an instant, everything changed. I was not alone. With sudden, inexplicable clarity and giddy relief, I realized that I didn't have to have the vocabulary or wisdom to communicate what I felt. I was profoundly aware of companionship—quiet, divine presence—whose own joy and delight matched mine. And I knew that words were not necessary for God to know how deeply grateful I was. The conviction that I was not alone in my joy and that my gratitude was acknowledged and understood magnified my sense of blessing while bestowing a deep and enveloping peace. I could simply continue to walk forward assured that every thought, word, and desire I had ever had was known and reverenced by God. Being in the presence of God is to have access to infinite vocabulary—precise and impeccable. It is to be radically understood. This was my first experience of prayer, and all of my life I have been struck by its genesis in joy.

There are many occasions when we pray out of desolation, regret, excruciating loss, intractable anxiety, and incomprehension for the suffering to which we bear witness. There is tremendous consolation in this. But to be in relationship with another—with God—means sharing our joys as well as our sorrows, our blessings and deepest loves as well as our vulnerabilities and failures.

I am reminded by my eight-year-old self to pray from a deep gratitude and joy for all the blessings of this life.

Anonymous Blessing in the Desert Labyrinth

At a desert monastery I had the opportunity to walk a labyrinth made of stones surrounded by exotic flora. I was completely alone, but far from lonely, enchanted by the mysterious beauty and contradiction of uninviting, captivating cacti amid the craggy landscape.

I wanted to empty myself of the accumulated cares and worries of ordinary life as I pursued the circuitous path marked by indigenous rock. With each step closer to the center, I offered the prayer I have prayed daily.

"Empty me of all that stands between You and me that I might be filled with Your imagination, desire, love, and will. Help me to be an effective instrument of all that You intend."

I exhaled worry and breathed in gratitude.

At the center of the labyrinth I took delight at the offerings other visitors had brought and left in supplication, remembrance, or thanksgiving. Small gifts of stone, a pencil, a tiny seashell far from home, a fortune cookie wisp proffering, "Be unconventional, even visionary." From the makeshift altar I took one white stone, smooth and cool, and as I retraced the winding path I prayed for the person who had left it. Knowing nothing of the life, challenges, hopes, or fears of the person for whom I was praying, I asked that he or she be granted a deep and abiding peace, experience gratitude, and know great love. I prayed for her fulfillment, for the concerns on his heart, for an answer to her own prayers.

> "Prayer is an act of love."
>
> —St. Teresa of Avila

I have since wondered about the value of such prayer.

It reminds me of anonymous philanthropy where the recipient receives an entirely unexpected financial gift and never learns the identity of the donor. Did the person I prayed for in the desert experience the gift? I will never know. But much as the philanthropist attests that it is she who benefits the most from serving others through generosity, I, too, was aware of a profound personal benefit that came as a consequence for praying for another. Since I did not know the identity of the person who left the smooth white stone, in a sense everyone became a candidate for my compassion and prayerful concern. And whether the person was a kindred soul or radically different, with opposing theological and political views, a completely different set of values or life experiences, he or she was the one for whom I committed to pray. I was invested in his or her fulfillment and peace and abundant blessing. This unconditional grace I asked God to lavish on my intimate stranger expanded my capacity to love and reminded me that all people, without exception, are part of the human family to which I belong, in need of care and blessing.

Now I make it a habit when beginning a new day, embarking upon a trip to a new part of the world, or attending a conference, to pray for the people I will meet for the first time, asking God to bless their lives, provide them encouragement, and scatter delight upon them. I pray for applicants who have yet to approach the Raskob Foundation or our sister foundations. I pray for donors I have not yet met who will invest in promising initiatives that strengthen the church and attend to the needs of a hurting world. I pray for the people my children will one day meet and fall in love with and spend their lives with. If I am sincere in my prayer, then I am already invested in blessing the lives of others, predisposed to meeting them with joyful expectation.

7

Enthusiasm and Delight

It Can Be Done. It Can Be Fun.

As I said in the first chapter, I was neither qualified nor eager for the role of director of development. The timing was terrible, and my ill-informed impressions of fundraising were shameful. In fact, I viscerally blanched at the thought of the responsibility. The task was presented as low-stress, part-time, entailing very little travel with a modest goal of "only" $5 million. None of which, of course, ended up being the case. Fr. Bob was persuasive, kind, and inexplicably certain that I was the right person for the role. When I did agree to work with him after five meaningful days of prayer, he was elated.

At which point the goal doubled to $10 million.

Three months into our work together, fueled by a passionate commitment to bring a Catholic intellectual and spiritual center of consequence to fruition, overwhelmed by the magnitude of work our aspirations would entail, sleep-deprived with a newborn at my constant ready, Fr. Bob—my prime collaborator—gave me a present. It was an elegant plaque that said, simply, IT CAN BE DONE.

It sat on my desk, a daily reminder of a truth to which we were both committed. Failure was not an option, for the beneficiaries of our effort were not us, but generations of students not yet even born. We were going to do this, and do this right the first time. We shared a sense of urgency. And as long as we were dedicating all of our energies to this pursuit, we were determined to aim for the highest levels of quality, creativity, and excellence in every aspect of our vision. Terrifying. But it can be done.

Unwavering conviction that it can be done is essential to success in any endeavor but is especially true for those aspirations deemed impossible.

I have cherished this first of many gifts from my extraordinary colleague and now lifelong friend. IT CAN BE DONE became our touchstone when all the odds seemed stacked against us, when the work became increasingly demanding, when obstacles appeared out of nowhere, erratic, unpredictable, and sometimes shocking. Knowing it can be done militates against the temptation to surrender or downgrade one's vision, to acquiesce to what others will insist are more realistic expectations.

> "In our deepest longings we hear echoes of God's longing for us. And the more we can follow these deep-down desires, those that God places within us for our happiness, the more joyful we will find ourselves."
>
> —James Martin, SJ

Of course, knowing it can be done is not, in and of itself, enough. There is also the necessity of hard work, the willingness to live by the maxim that much can be accomplished when no one cares who gets the credit, an indefatigable tenacity, and a genuine fidelity to purpose.

But there is one other essential quality, often overlooked or disregarded.

This time it was my turn to offer him a gift. For Christmas I wrapped and presented an equally elegant, equally instructive plaque that said, IT CAN BE FUN.

Anything worth accomplishing is worth accomplishing well. The bigger the vision, the more demanding the task. Bringing potential to fruition is not for the faint of heart. But right in the midst of the arduous demands of the task is the chance, indeed the requirement, to bring joy to the endeavor. We learned to celebrate often. We celebrated small steps, triumphant accomplishments, mistakes along the way, and the sheer privilege of lending our lives to something larger than ourselves. We looked for reasons to be glad. We focused on the present and what we could do now that would bring future beneficence to others. We sought to find the humor in many situations. We lived out of conscious gratitude. We took delight in people we met, adventures we had,

> "Scientists have discovered that the small, brave act of cooperating with another person, of choosing trust over cynicism, generosity over selfishness, makes the brain light up with quiet joy."
>
> —Natalie Angier

and ideas that surfaced, regarding all as essential pieces of the mosaic being wrought through diligent labor.

Confidence and joyful passion are an irresistible combination. It can be done, and it can be fun.

Joy

When I attended Yale Divinity School, some of the most brilliant, dedicated, compassionate students I knew were Roman Catholic women. Many of them went on to serve as pastoral associates and lay ecclesial ministers in parishes across the United States. One, Mary Ellen O'Driscoll, is a very close friend, a superbly gifted spiritual adviser, deeply reflective and prayerful, a woman who loves the church and anguishes when it fails to live up to or merely approximate the ideal. She was hired to work in a Catholic parish that was especially vibrant, and she had enormous respect for the pastor and her colleagues on the pastoral team. Together they worked hard to engage parishioners to model with them a faith community in which they could take great pride and from which draw great nourishment.

I saw my classmate soon after she returned from a vacation that took her out of state and provided her the opportunity to visit diverse parishes for Mass. It was not all delight. In fact she reported that on one occasion the Mass was so lackluster, with the celebrant going through the motions as if by rote, no intonation, a poorly crafted homily, entirely joyless. The lack of affect was so distracting, she confided to me, that Mass came dangerously close to being an occasion of sin for her! So distressed was she by the somber, emotionless timbre, she confessed that she wanted to approach the pastor at the conclusion of the Mass and say, "Father, I realize this is the Holy Sacrifice of the Mass, but you are not the one being sacrificed!"

Joy has an infectious quality to it. Joy is constitutive of the Gospel and of living an authentic life of faith. And it is impossible to be a good steward of the potential at hand if one does not cultivate a joyful heart, attitude, and disposition.

In 2011, anticipating the birth of the seven billionth person, our creative friend, Valerie Belanger, conceived of a global art installation centered on one question: "What would you say to the 7 billionth person?"

The answers, in a variety of media, fell along a spectrum: alarming, anxious prognostication about the dire state of the world into which this child would be born, on one end, and heartfelt, hopeful joy for a child we have been waiting to welcome, on the other.

Where would your response fall?

People of faith are instructed to bear joy and to bear witness to joy even in the midst of oppression, suffering, poverty, and brokenheartedness. This is not facile joy, but joy that comes from faith—faith in God and faith in something larger than oneself. It is a spiritual discipline to cultivate. Faith that it is possible to make a meaningful difference in the lives of others. Faith that it is possible to correct unjust structures. Faith that it is possible to eliminate extreme poverty and inequality. Faith that it is possible to ensure potable water for all people. Faith that peace can be achieved, that reconciliation can be effected, that forgiveness can be extended.

Life is hard. It can be crushing. Poverty, environmental degradation, violence. We experience injustice and can be our own oppressors with our negative thoughts and our temptations to despair. Vulnerable people are abused, and powerful people protect institutions before children. It is not fair that women and girls suffer disproportionately the effects of war and poverty and disease. It is not acceptable that whole populations in parts of the world are subject to abject famine or have no access to clean water. The dignity of the human person is made a mockery of when we hurt or degrade each other because of race, religion, ethnicity, politics, sexual orientation, or gender. Love dies. Loved ones die. Relationships end. Meaningful chapters of our lives conclude, and emptiness, loneliness, regret, and sorrow can be excruciating. How in the midst of communal and personal suffering can one access joy, let alone radiate it? It seems incongruous, if not impossible.

I understand, therefore, why some of the submissions for our friend's art installation depicted scenes of violence, hunger, toxicity, human trafficking, and genocide, alerting the seven billionth person to the kind of world she or he will find.

Christianity's response to the suffering of life is an incarnational God. That God took on human form entering so intimately into our experience, suffering, dying, and rising is the source of Christian joy. Our task as baptized members is to bear witness to that joy, even in the midst of sorrow.

Scripture provides advice to cultivate such joy.

In 1 Thessalonians 5:16-18, St. Paul instructs us to "Rejoice always, pray without ceasing, give thanks in all circumstances." Life does not have to be perfect for us to find reasons to be grateful. In the midst of tremendous human suffering, there can be found compassion, mercy, altruism, and love. Be aware of such grace and human kindness. It is everywhere, even and especially when there is concomitant human anguish and loss. Rejoice in this. *Pray without ceasing.* Prayer done well changes the one who is praying. It cracks open our minds, liberates us from the oppression of our thoughts and mental habits, turns our minds to a new way of seeing, radically alters our perspective, allows us to see God in our midst. Prayer is designed to bring us closer to God and all that God intends for us. *Give thanks in all circumstances.* Gratitude begets gratitude. Blessings multiply. And the fruit of the habit of gratitude is that soon one experiences blessing where before one experienced only lament.

These are not easy spiritual habits, but they are hallmarks of the Christian life. It is our responsibility to cultivate, evince, bear witness to, and share the joy that comes from knowing—truly knowing—God is present right here.

When we bear witness to joy, we offer hope to a broken world. And the world needs hope.

By our very lives, we can be the bearers of hope and joy. It is a good way to be: to live in such a way that everyone who knows you sees that in God is the joy of your soul, and this joy is their inheritance, too.

That's not a bad message to welcome all new people born to our world.

Grace under Pressure

The Thomas E. Golden, Jr. Center, the formal name of the Catholic Center at Yale, is more than seven years old as I write this book, enveloped in the warmth of the fire in the reading room of the library made possible by Fay Vincent and named in memory of his father who was an early student leader in the Catholic community while at Yale. It is my favorite building, a symbol of faith, tenacity, hard work, and mission. It is entirely different to look back from this vantage point, knowing the tangible concrete success of the effort. At the start of the effort it seemed impossible, and most people affirmed how impossible it would be. On our darkest days, tempted to despair and accede to the negative views expressed by smart and accomplished people, it was especially important to cultivate an inner joy and confidence. We needed to personify grace under pressure.

The stakes were high. The board after all had, with great hesitation, signed on for a $5 million capital campaign originally. The final goal was fifteen times that amount. Our architect was the world-class and world-famous Cesar Pelli. The Corporation of Yale University had agreed to lease us significant property adjacent to Saint Thomas More Chapel to construct a 30,000-square-foot student center. Our conviction was that the most important part of our effort was to demonstrate that campus ministry at Yale was worthy of generosity. Toward that end easily 75 percent of my time was spent on programmatic development. We did not want to stop advancing our mission in order to raise money so that we could then resume advancing the mission. If the mission was urgent, compelling, and worthy, which it was, we couldn't afford to wait.

> "Joy is really the simplest form of gratitude."
>
> —Karl Barth

Each time the board met I was invited to give a report. Each time I began by speaking about the expanded programmatic offerings we were introducing and how wide a net we were casting to attract young adults of all persuasions, backgrounds, and levels of catechesis. I drew attention to how our public profile was being elevated, how many more students were participating every day of the week, and how much money we had raised. Already we had raised three times the original goal. But the goal kept increasing, and our ability to meet that goal became more and more arduous.

I found myself in a conundrum. The only way I knew how to do my job well was to passionately, confidently highlight all of the signs of growth and vitality, the result of our comprehensive strategy to be mission and program driven and to be worthy of profound generosity. But as the stakes grew and the time elapsed, despite the overwhelming signs of new life and vitality, our board was exercising their fiduciary responsibility and properly wanting me to focus my remarks on only one detail: how much money had been raised since the board last met.

At some point every development director experiences this profound frustration and disappointment about the pace of fundraising, whether internally or externally. One can and should be methodical and detailed about setting goals and measuring progress, including points of contact, personal calls and visits, grant proposal submissions, annual appeals, and specific asks. But the one detail that cannot be controlled is when a donor will commit to the investment.

Against this backdrop I offer this story.

It is the eve of our board meeting. I am up late, long after I have put my two children to sleep. I am working in my home office. I begin with prayer and look at the beautiful collection of handcrafted crucifixes hanging on the wall above my desk. I implore God to give me the ability, composure, grace, élan, and words to keep our board engaged and confident. Losing their confidence in the vision of where we are heading would be disastrous for our momentum. I have very good news to report, but it is nearly all related to programmatic accomplishments. For example, so many students have been drawn into the ministry that we have added a third Sunday liturgy, at 10:00 p.m., and it is a great success.

"God, help me to be an effective communicator of the value of perseverance. Give me the words to encourage the members of the board in this important pursuit. Help me to exude the confidence I draw from knowing this is important, meaningful, faith-filled work. What is it, God, that I might say to relieve their anxiety, encourage their confidence, inspire their own continued generosity?"

And it was at that precise moment that the phone in my home office rang. Odd, since it was very late on a Friday night.

"Hello, this is Kerry Robinson."

Calling was a Yale alumnus from the West Coast who was in his eighties. We had never met. He quickly and politely explained that he and his wife had been following all of the exciting programmatic developments occurring at Saint Thomas More Chapel at Yale, and they had just been discussing how exciting the expansion was, the elevation of Catholic intellectual life, the increased number of students participating in the life of the church, and the social justice programs we were introducing. So impressed were they by the *programmatic accomplishments* that they had decided to make a donation of $1 million to our campaign, and he was calling to let me know of their desire to support us.

To which I replied, "Is this God?"

I quickly regained my composure and in a rush of excitement began to explain that it was the eve of our board meeting and I had just been praying for the words to share with our board the next day when the phone rang and this was the most incredibly supportive, generous, perfectly timed sign of grace in all that we have been bringing to life on Yale's campus. He went on to say, "We are so impressed, in fact, by the approach Fr. Bob, the staff, the board, and you have taken, that we would be just as happy to have you decide how best to use the million-dollar gift. It is entirely unrestricted. We trust your judgment about how best it can be used."

I was stunned.

And then the most remarkable part of the conversation occurred. As I began to thank him profusely for this most consequential of gifts, the largest gift we had received to date, free of all restrictions, he gently interrupted me and said, "Don't thank us, Kerry. You make it a joy to give."

When I recounted this exchange with my wonderful husband, Michael, who had so patiently supported and encouraged me throughout every demanding day and night of the development effort, he quipped, "You might not want to broadcast that last comment too widely. If you are doing your job properly, aren't they supposed to give till it hurts?"

Rejoicing in the Good Fortune of Others

I was fortunate to learn a crucially important life lesson the easy way: I was a child, and it came naturally.

The lesson is this: cultivate the habit of taking delight in the good fortune of others and you will never be without occasion for joy.

One evening after school, my father asked how my day was. My reply was an enthusiastic litany of wonderful news befalling various classmates and teachers and friends of friends, none of which involved me personally but all of which signified accolades or much-longed-for gifts or news of promised travel to come for others in my close proximity. I remember feeling genuine happiness and anticipation on their behalf until my father interrupted my vicarious reverie with an observation I have never forgotten. He told me that it was very rare and highly unusual for a person to evince such unadulterated and energetic happiness on behalf of the good fortune of others. He said he marveled at my childlike capacity, that such a disposition was a gift and that he hoped I never lost the habit, especially as I grew into adulthood.

> "When you act like God, you get to feel like God."
>
> —Ron Rolheiser, OMI

I was stunned. It seemed, from my very young perspective, completely counterintuitive. How could it be rare to be happy for others? Good news, like its opposite, was daily fare. Was there any other response to good news than delight, even as an entirely selfless expression? And it made me wary of adulthood, determined to ward off and resist the evident seduction of jadedness and jealousy.

The more I pondered my father's curious response, the more I was determined to heed his advice to cultivate the habit. It was, after all, the best guarantee for an other-centered, expansive life. It was the best defense against *schadenfreude*, the most ignoble of human responses. And it was the best predictor that regardless of the hand that life might deal me, replete with disappointment, failure, and heartache, I would never be without a reason for joy on behalf of someone, somewhere.

The older I become, the more valuable has been this habit. It is not always easy, particularly when another's good fortune—public accolade, requited love, promotion, dream come true—seems to be at one's own expense. But life is not a zero-sum game. Happiness begets happiness; misery begets misery. And it is impossible to know the sacrifices others have made for their success or, for that matter, to know what others truly endure and carry in their lives. Nothing is ever as it appears on the surface. There is astonishing personal suffering to which no one is immune for long. Given these realities, the choice to celebrate good news and good fortune, accomplishment and success, wherever one finds it, is always the wise choice.

I often wonder if I might have outgrown the habit had my father not intervened with his assessment from an experienced, adult perspective. My good fortune is that he did, while I was still so young, and that I trusted his wisdom and insight enough to act upon it. Cultivating this habit has brought a steady diet of delight into my life. And it has helped me to avoid occasions of regret, envy, bitterness, and parsimony of the heart.

Regardless of the circumstances, when the choice is between generosity of spirit or jealous self-pity, there is only one life-giving option leading to freedom. Why be complicit in the world's economy of joy? Participate in delight. Whose good fortune will you celebrate today?

Habit of Happiness—A Little Awe and Enthusiasm

One morning I woke to a voluminous moon at a retreat center in northern Florida after presenting to priests from eleven dioceses on the spirituality of fundraising.

Before anyone else was awake, I took leave of the tranquil center and set out for the Atlantic Ocean in order to walk the beach at sunrise.

I have spent at least one week of every year of my life at the beach in any number of houses on the edge of the ocean. There is no more replenishing, soulfully familiar place for me on earth.

Five generations of women, and the men we love, have enjoyed this family tradition, marked by the sign of conviviality. Books are read, walks are taken, games are played, riotously funny stories are retold, and lavish meals are shared. The ocean lends itself to meaningful discussion and discernment at every stage of life.

Once, with the entire extended family present, a deliberate conversation ensued about the secret of happiness.

A young cousin volunteered that the secret to attain happiness is to resist its pursuit and allow it to manifest itself. An aunt instructed: be present to the moment, aware and appreciative. Another suggested we take an inventory of all that our week together at the beach comprised and consider that the magic recipe. My brother was specific,

"A Super Bowl championship for my team." We agreed that happiness has an elusive quality, that there are likely many avenues to its encounter, that all responses had personal authenticity, each one worthy of deeper consideration and attempt.

The only one who had not spoken was my grandmother, Martha Enck Loftin. It was the last time as a family gathered at the beach that we would enjoy the company of this vibrant, exceedingly joyful, vivacious woman; these were her final weeks of life. We pressed her for an answer to the question "What is the secret to happiness?" It was frankly hard to imagine anyone more adept at a response;

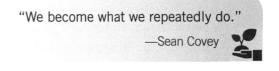

"We become what we repeatedly do."

—Sean Covey

her easy delight in all things, her indomitable positive outlook, and her laughter's cadence were chief among her defining characteristics. So when she demurred and said that she didn't believe she had anything to add, no real secret, no magic formula for us to grasp, we were collectively disappointed and unsettled. We wanted to be more like her, a bona fide *bonne vivante*. If only we knew her secret. We begged her for an answer, arguing that she exemplified in her very disposition that which we were seeking. Surely she had some clue to extend, we earnestly entreated.

Despite labored breathing presaging her final days of life, she said softly, smiling, as though it had only just occurred to her that this might in fact be relevant, "I do try to start each day with a little awe and enthusiasm."

After she died, I held these words with reverence and tried to wake each morning with the same commitment, if only to honor her memory. I soon found merit in the exercise, benefit to the habit. There is a marked difference between beginning a day dissatisfied—with dread, weariness, fear, inertia, or boredom—and welcoming morning consciousness with its opposite. We are apt to see what we are looking for, to encounter what we expect, and to validate what we feel as the day proceeds.

This morning I got to watch the moon set and the sun rise on a spectacularly beautiful beach. Nature's prodigal daily gift rendered me speechless with gratitude to be witness to such aesthetic majesty. How easy to greet this day with awe and enthusiasm.

How much easier still when doing so has been made effortless by practice.

Forming Children in Lives of Stewardship

Every year on the eve of my children's birthdays, it is the same.

I enter my child's room, sit on the edge of the bed, and marvel at the miracle that is silently asleep before me. Quietly, trying not to disturb such peaceful slumber, I say softly, "We have been waiting our whole lives for you. There is no one on earth like you. You are deeply loved. To be your mother is a profound blessing. You are a gift to Daddy and to me, to our family, to your friends, and to all who know you. You are cherished beyond measure."

In the evening stillness of the room, I proceed with precision born of intimacy and name aloud my child's endearing, quintessential qualities. I speak of all he or she has received by virtue of simple circumstance of birth in a particular time and place. I emphasize the limitless possibility to do and to be anything their hearts desire over the course of their lifetimes. They have both ability and freedom to be teacher, president, rock star, artist, caregiver, poet, financier, architect, journalist. I remind my son and daughter that "to whom much has been given, much will be required" (Luke 12:48) and that while they can do anything with their lives, there is one condition they must honor for a life of meaning and value: make this world better, not worse. Contribute to the lives of others. Ennoble. Strengthen. Bless.

> "The ultimate test of a moral society is the kind of world that it leaves to its children."
>
> —Dietrich Bonhoeffer

I prepare to leave with kisses I have offered every day of their lives. "Happy Birthday. I love you all the much."

Every year it is the same. My children, clearly asleep at the start of the annual ritual monologue, slowly wake but pretend to remain asleep—body still, breathing soft, eyes closed. All that betrays them are the irrepressible smiles as they hear over and over again how extraordinarily, unreservedly loved they are.

Development Is Ministry

Fr. Bob and I met Tom Golden, the man for whom we would name the Catholic Center at Yale, on the day we boldly announced a multimillion dollar fundraising campaign. We were inexperienced but passionate about our vision of a Catholic intellectual and spiritual center of excellence that would raise the bar of Catholic campus ministry nationally. In our naïveté and ignorance of fundraising rules of thumb, we inadvertently broke most. We never conducted a feasibility study, and we announced the capital campaign before even one dollar had been raised, silently or loudly! We often wonder what impact a feasibility study would have had on our efforts. We cannot imagine such a study concluding that we would be able to raise $75 million.

We needed an occasion to bring alumni back to campus and to the Catholic Chapel. For our development efforts to succeed, it was necessary to reestablish contact with Catholic alumni who had been lost from the database. This was important for more than purposes of asking alumni for money. Catholic alumni dating back to the 1930s were part of the institutional memory of the Center. They were an integral part of the rich history of the ministry upon which we were building. We had little recourse to reclaiming their contact information, much less their attention, other than to create incentives for alumni to return to campus and take out advertisements in Catholic periodicals and local papers welcoming their return. We decided to mark the sixtieth anniversary of the dedication of Saint Thomas More Chapel with a weekend celebration and a daylong symposium entitled, "The Legacy of Thomas More: Catholic Faith and Intellectual Life at the Threshold of the 21st Century." Tom had not been back to campus in decades, but he was drawn to the speakers, including Monika Hellwig, Fr. Bryan Hehir, Paul Kennedy, Louis Dupré, and William F. Buckley, Jr.

Tom's presence was the first sign of how important the connection between elevating the visibility of the ministry and successful fundraising is. Despite what we would later come to appreciate—that Tom almost never ventured out to public events alone—there he was in attendance, seated unobtrusively in the back row, among the very first to express his interest in helping us bring our vision of a Catholic intellectual and spiritual center of consequence to fruition.

To our credit and no doubt to Tom's chagrin, it was years before we ever knew that this modestly dressed and humble man with a tiny, messy office was a person of such affluence. What drew us to each other was his faith in our vision. Thus began a thirteen-year profoundly intimate friendship with a profoundly private man. To witness Tom laugh, even as he lay dying, to see him well up with tears, even at his most fulfilled: these were sacred apertures to his essence and revealed an emotional and relational depth rarely visible on the surface.

Years after we first met, as Tom lay dying, he told Fr. Bob and me that we were family to him. He had never married and had no brothers and sisters. At the celebration of his funeral Mass, Fr. Bob preached and I delivered the eulogy. The opportunity to participate in such a prominent way was Tom's final gift to us. He was family to us, too.

There is this funny thing about grace: it is always experienced as mutual. It is never expected. It comes in remarkably unpredictable manners and forms. And if you allow it, grace, like love, cracks open wide your heart, transforming everything for the good.

Tom's involvement in the development effort and in our lives had a profound and lasting impact. Years after we befriended Tom, he signed a testamentary agreement, promising to leave $25 million or 75 percent of his estate—whichever was greater—to Saint Thomas More Chapel when he died.

He had conditions, the first of which was that we continue to encourage other Catholic alumni to contribute to the construction of the building. He wanted to see the building in his lifetime, so time was of the essence. When we had succeeded in raising $25 million for the building fund from Yale Catholic alumni, built and dedicated the building, and obtained a certificate of occupancy, we would have the security of knowing that at least $25 million would be left to Saint Thomas More Chapel. This gift would support the expanded operating costs of the ministry, as well as ongoing maintenance of the new facility. The long-term financial health of the chaplaincy would be provided. This first condition we welcomed because it established a gravitas and timeline for our efforts. It put our "feet to the fire."

"Asking people for money is giving them the opportunity to put their resources at the disposal of [advancing the Reign of God]."

—Henri Nouwen

Tom's second condition we welcomed with even greater enthusiasm because he was our close friend and we cared for him deeply: he wanted us to pray for him—that he live a very long life. He promised with remarkable self-confidence that each year of life he lived would only mean that the assets of his estate would grow, and therefore 75 percent promised to Saint Thomas More Chapel would grow to far more than $25 million.

Once, on Easter, Tom joined us for Mass in the Chapel. The highpoint of our liturgical calendar, this was a perfect spring day. The flowers were overflowing in the sanctuary. The music was exceptional; the homily outstanding. The Chapel was full to overflowing with students, faculty, and families. It was standing room only. My husband, Michael, and I sat with Tom near the front and I noticed that throughout the entire liturgy Tom was quietly weeping. Knowing how private he was, I did not draw attention to this, but I was struck by how evidently moved he was by the liturgy. At the conclusion of Mass, as we processed out of the Chapel and into the abundant sunshine, I thanked him for coming, for choosing this sacred place on this sacred day. I told him his presence was a blessing to us.

Very quietly he said, "I probably should not confess this to you, Kerry, but this is my first Mass in over forty years."

I was stunned. And suddenly it was crystal clear that even if we had not so much as raised ten dollars in this development effort, we had at least succeeded in reconciling this man with his God and with his faith community. After I wished him a Happy Easter and saw him to his car, I went running to Fr. Bob and announced, "I told you it was ministry!"

Tom lived to see the new center, dedicated in his honor, and every year on the Golden Center's birthday, which by sheer accident of grace was my birthday too, he and I would celebrate together over lunch. We enjoyed that happy tradition for five years before his sorrowful passing.

How do you explain that this frugal, cerebral, rational, hardworking man made the decision he did, to give so much away, in order to bring a vision of Catholic life at Yale to fruition that he would never live to see fully realized?

Despite his yearning to touch what was real, to have tangible proof, to cast his lot in favor of concrete, material reality, in the end Tom's generosity was never solely about a building. It was about faith in the value of credible, intellectual, and spiritual ministry. Faith in young adults, students, and future generations. Tom's leap of faith was ultimately in others. He believed that students, by participating in Catholic life at Yale, would be formed, inspired, and sustained in an adult mature faith so consequential that they would live lives of magnanimity and hope, courage, and mercy in service to this broken world. He believed in precisely the vision we espoused.

Donors Are Subjects, not Objects

In the course of the development effort, one lesson above all influenced our ability to be effective. We learned the lesson the hard way: by confronting multiple perceived obstacles to our success with honesty and candor. I was working with an inspiring, charismatic, engaging, faith-filled Catholic priest. I admired the dedication and hours he put into preparing beautiful, intelligent homilies. I stood in awe of his pastoral sensitivity. I marveled at his spiritual gift for making other people through pastoral counseling sessions see themselves the way God must see them, that is, with mercy and an endless reservoir of love and compassion. Fr. Bob could be alternately wise, funny, self-deprecating, humble, and commanding. He got along with people of all ages, backgrounds, and experiences. I remember telling him once that he is so gifted in his ability to relate pastorally to others that he is

"Candor is a compliment; it implies equality. It's how true friends talk."

—Peggy Noonan

not even aware of how strong the gift he possesses is. A pastoral encounter with Fr. Bob was like having a mirror held up to your soul and what you saw reflected back was how God saw you: the truest, most beautiful, most authentic core of who you were.

And yet, when I would take him on the road to meet with prospective donors, everything changed. He appeared distracted, subdued, nervous, and distant. It was clear he didn't want to be there, in the meeting. I couldn't understand it, and we spent some time confronting this challenge. What we realized was that we were unwittingly viewing donors as objects to try to get as much money from as quickly and painlessly as possible, rather than as subjects in their own right. Donor prospects are not objects; they are subjects, and like all of us, they want to contribute to something meaningful and life-giving and successful. Like us, they too search for meaning, have fears and hopes, desires and regrets, and beliefs that should be acknowledged and reverenced.

As soon as we realized this fundamental truth, everything changed. Understanding donor prospects as subjects in their own right allowed for the conversations to be what all of Fr. Bob's pastoral conversations were: intimate, sacred, relational occasions. Now Fr. Bob could bring his full self to the task and look forward to meeting prospective donors. Gone was any semblance of cognitive dissonance. Now he could be effortless and natural in every occasion. That is to say, he was joyful, attentive, confident, passionate, genuinely interested in the donor's perspective and hopes, tremendously at ease.

And it meant we could enter into the joys, hopes, regrets, and sorrows of the people we were visiting far more intimately, to far more meaningful effect.

On Reverencing Sorrow

I knew how much my mother loved me by the way in which she addressed my sorrow. She never dismissed my emotions; she acknowledged and validated the kaleidoscope of human experience.

One evening, when I was a very young girl, she found me crying in my room. Sitting on the side of my bed, she told me how sorry she was that I was feeling sad. And then she said something extraordinary. She told me that she wished she had a beautiful crystal vial to collect and save every one of my tears. As she spoke to me, she gathered each slowing tear from my cheek onto her finger, held it to the light, and said, "These are such beautiful tears. I cherish every part of you."

> "A true friend sees the first tear . . . catches the second . . . and stops the third."
>
> —Angelique Arnauld

It was, years later, one of many maternal lessons I carried into my own experience of parenthood. From the earliest ages, my children knew how much I reverenced all that their lives contained. With great care I would collect their tears on my finger, repeating what my mother had said to me: "These are such beautiful tears. I wish that I could save such precious tears in an exquisite crystal vial."

Neither my children nor I can recall the cause of our sorrow in any given example, but we do remember being cherished and consoled. We remember the sense of reverence and nobility conferred on ordinary experience. We remember being taken seriously and being loved at our most vulnerable.

I imagine God to be like this: perfectly maternal, intimate witness to our joys and sorrows, falling in love with us more deeply with every example of our raw vulnerability, enveloping us with her confidence that all will be well.

When we enter into sacred discussion with donors or grantees or beneficiaries of a ministry, vulnerability is established. Donors, grantees, and beneficiaries need each other to bring something beautiful and life-giving to fruition. It is a collaboration borne of deep desire to find meaning, to be a blessing, to be part of something successful and consequential, and to heal the sorrows of life.

Listening and Silence

A crucial component of an authentic relationship with another person is the quality of our capacity to listen. The more frenetic our lives, the more ways for people to contact us, the more interruptions to our focus, the harder it is to be in the present and to be attentive to the people with whom we are. In establishing any relationship, it is vital to be present to one another, and this means to listen, actively.

And when it comes to raising money and asking a prospective donor to make a financial investment, it is especially important to remember how to listen and to fight the temptation to fill any moments of silence.

Fr. Bob and I practiced the entire flight from Hartford, Connecticut, to Chicago, Illinois. We agreed that it would be Fr. Bob who made the formal request to the Yale Catholic alumnus we were meeting for lunch. We had met the alumnus many times before, had a very good relationship with him, and credited him for giving the board confidence to begin a capital campaign in the first place. In Fr. Bob's first year of his chaplaincy, Mr. Thomas Mints had returned to campus for his reunion. After Mass Sunday morning at Saint Thomas More Chapel, Mr. Mints asked Fr. Bob if there was anything he needed. Fr. Bob replied that the roof of the Chapel had recently begun to leak and what was needed was a roof repair. Mr. Mints told Fr. Bob not to worry, that he would send some shares of stock to put toward the repair.

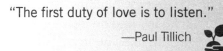

"The first duty of love is to listen."

—Paul Tillich

A few weeks later the stock arrived. To Fr. Bob's astonishment, it totaled $57,000. It was the first time Fr. Bob realized that there were alumni for whom the Chapel mattered and who might be willing, like Mr. Mints, to support a development effort.

We never ceased reminding Mr. Mints about his unwitting catalytic role, and we were always grateful. He was a wonderful conversationalist, full of ideas and suggestions on how we could expand Catholic life at Yale.

Now we were flying to Chicago to meet him for lunch, and we were prepared to ask him for a million dollars for our building fund.

Again and again, on the flight, we practiced. I pretended I was the donor. Fr. Bob delivered his request with perfection. Each time I would remind him that the single most important part of the request was to stop speaking as soon as he delivered the words "We would like you to consider a gift of one million dollars." I impressed upon him how difficult it would seem at the time. There would necessarily be a pause in the conversation. That silence would seem interminable, even painful. But it was absolutely critical that he not try to fill the void with more discussion. Allow Mr. Mints to respond. Even if he says no, we will have learned something. But let him answer, I advised.

Lunch was vibrant and joyful. We were with our longtime friend, the very first person to support our development efforts. He was in great shape and good spirits. We spent most of the lunch updating him on the progress of our programmatic expansion, the total dollars raised in various categories, the plans under way for groundbreaking on the new building. And then as the check was brought to Mr. Mints, who insisted on treating us, Fr. Bob took a deep breath and said, "We would like you to consider a gift of one million dollars."

Perfect.

Except Fr. Bob immediately followed with, "Of course you are going to want to discuss this with your wife, and if that is too large a sum, you and your wife might consider a smaller amount. It could also be pledged over three or even five years. Take your time to think about. No need to give us your answer now."

And Mr. Mints, preoccupied with signing the bill, never said a word.

Raising Money. Selling Cars.

Years ago, a well-respected executive and I were asked to provide advice to a group of leaders who wanted to expand Catholic life at another prominent secular university and knew they would need to be highly successful at raising money in order to do so. The executive had wonderful expertise to draw upon and was particularly helpful to them in outlining various considerations involving property, administration, financial management, and legal contractual relationships. And then she was asked a question about how they might go about being as effective as possible in raising money for the effort.

She said, "Raising money is a lot like selling cars. The first thing I will do when you walk into my showroom is persuade you to give me your car keys. I will lock them in a drawer in my office and keep you in my showroom for as long as possible. I know you are interested in buying a car. You have come to my dealership. It is in my best interest to keep you in my dealership for as long as possible. I know that the longer you invest your time in my showroom, the greater the likelihood that you will wind up buying one of my cars. You will perform the cost analysis in your head, and having already invested a great amount of your time, that is precious, you will not want to cut your losses so easily. Eventually, if held hostage long enough, you will buy a car from me."

I was completely dumbfounded.

The audience nodded and seemed to understand her point. And although I have remembered for many years this conversation and my own surprise at the analogy, I am willing to concede that she may have made a valid psychological observation. The problem is that giving out of obligation, or worse, as a consequence of willful manipulation, will never issue in the kind of investment genuinely being sought. This might be an expedient tactic to raise some money, but it violates the principle of neighbor love, of seeing a donor prospect as a subject, not an object, of entering into a relationship of mutual respect and of genuine invitation.

Qualities to Seek in a Development Director

People often ask what qualities they should look for in a development director. I heard a man once give an answer to this question before I had ever had any direct experience of development myself, and all these years later I remember his answer and find it to be absolutely accurate. He said, "I look for three things: the ability to speak and write well; the ability to take initiative; and enthusiasm for the mission."

The ability to speak and write well, to communicate with a wide diversity of others, was a particularly valuable quality for our development efforts. It was not only that we wanted to enter into deep and meaningful conversations with Yale Catholic alumni, students, parents, faculty, and friends of the Chapel. We also wanted to appeal to Catholic luminaries in a compelling way, extending invitations to them to visit campus, to offer lectures, to meet students, and to add to the reputation of our ministry.

One guest we were eager to invite was Fr. Richard Rohr, OFM, spiritual writer extraordinaire. I had met him while on retreat at the Center for Action and Contemplation that he founded in Albuquerque, New Mexico, and was enchanted. When I happened to speak to him again, he suggested that he would be glad to speak at Yale but that I should have Fr. Bob write him an official letter of invitation so it could be added to his master calendar. When he found himself in New England next, he would be sure to come to Yale. I was elated and immediately set about writing a letter to Fr. Richard in Fr. Bob's name. We had a long-standing practice (and joke) that I, in Fr. Bob's name, would draft correspondence to speakers or donors, hoping they would agree to our requests, then Fr. Bob would eliminate all adjectives, I would put them back in, and we would get the YES!

"There are some people who have the quality of richness and joy in them and they communicate it to everything they touch. It is first of all a physical quality; then it is a quality of the spirit."

—Tom Wolfe

As fate would have it, I had an occasion to meet Fr. Richard in person shortly after the letter was sent. I confess to being starstruck. I had read everything he had published, had benefited enormously by being on retreat with him, and here I was in the privileged encounter of sharing a meal with him. All I wanted to do was make a good impression! Always advancing the mission of Catholic life at Yale, I impressed upon him how grateful we were that he was considering including Yale in his upcoming travels. I added, "And you will really enjoy meeting my colleague, Fr. Bob Beloin."

Fr. Richard replied, "Oh, Kerry! You do not need to tell me that. I cannot WAIT to meet him. Do you know he sent me the most beautifully written, spiritually astute, warm, loving, encouraging, and affirming letter I may have ever received! What a great man he surely is! I can't wait to spend time with him."

Fr. Bob loves to tell this story to anyone who will listen.

By far the most demanding part of my set of responsibilities for the capital campaign was taking the days on the calendar that we had set aside for development travel and calling Yale Catholic alumni, who were never expecting my call, in order to fill our itinerary. I had to be 100 percent on: good energy in my voice and demeanor, joyful, confident, easygoing, enthusiastic . . . no matter what kind of day I was actually having or how little sleep the babies had allowed me the previous night. On this particular occasion, I had left the door to my office open, and as Fr. Bob walked past, he overheard me say to a prospective donor I was hoping would agree to see us in Los Angeles the following month, "You will really enjoy meeting Fr. Bob. He is the most remarkable chaplain. Students adore him. He has an exquisite pastoral disposition. He is one of the very best homilists I have ever known, a great leader and visionary, with a fabulous sense of humor. Just a terrific man all around!" Happily, I secured the appointment for us, hung up the phone feeling very proud of myself, and found Fr. Bob looking at me with a grim expression.

"Kerry, you can't describe me in those glowing, superlative terms. They will be so disappointed when they actually meet me!"

Relieved it was not something more serious and without missing a beat, I replied, "Oh, I already have that all figured out. I am just going to tell them as an aside that you are feeling a little under the weather when we get there."

Exciting the Philanthropic Imagination

There was enormous pressure on us to raise many millions of dollars as quickly as possible. Tom's testamentary gift was predicated on an ambitious timeline of construction so that he could see the building in his lifetime. We welcomed the condition; failure was not an option. The challenge with this was that it only served to increase the anxiety the board felt about the amount of money still to be raised, the timeline for raising it, and who would contribute.

In the midst of this, Fr. Bob and I found ourselves at a promising appointment in New York with a very accomplished, affluent, generous alumnus. We were treated to a stunning vista from his penthouse office overlooking Central Park and began to share our vision for Catholic life at Yale. He was deeply interested and exceedingly courteous, but over the course of the conversation, it became abundantly clear that our capital campaign, the building, the expanded program, and the endowment for campus ministry was not his primary philanthropic interest. Rather, what he seemed acutely interested in supporting were efforts that helped to break the cycle of poverty in families by providing quality education to poor elementary, middle, and high school students. He spoke with great concern and passion about this. He was at his most animated and eloquent when describing his hope to make a difference in the lives of this population of children.

The conversation returned to the expansion of Catholic life at Yale, the programs we had introduced, the increased participation of undergrads and grads, the amount of money we had raised, and plans for the new building. I can remember making a conscious decision that I feared would be a tremendous disappointment to our board if they were privy to my innermost thoughts, and likely to be surprising if not worrisome to Fr. Bob. The decision was abruptly to halt the conversation about our fundraising effort to benefit Yale and direct the conversation back to his primary philanthropic passion, the education of poor children.

Drawing from my familiarity and experience with foundations that I knew had an interest in supporting Catholic education and poverty-relief interventions, I began to describe to him not only specific schools, educational networks, and programs aimed at achieving the very goals he shared but also offered to introduce him to like-minded philanthropists from around the country. I was acutely aware that in doing so I was taking our prospective donor further away from investing in our capital campaign and risking instead that his investment would be directed at other nonprofits. I could only imagine what my board would have to say about this decision. I was worried, too, that by diverting attention away from our effort and onto the donor's primary charitable interest that I had effectively wasted Fr. Bob's time and undercut his primary goal in coming to Manhattan at the expense of time spent on pastoral ministry with students.

Every one of these thoughts I considered, but I took the risk because, quite simply, it was the right thing to do, especially if we viewed development as a ministry to donors. We were called to be attentive to him, to listen to what motivates him, come to know what he cares about and where he believes he could make a meaningful difference in the lives of others. Our role was to be responsive to the expressed hopes, concerns, desires, and interests of the donor. If those hopes and desires happened to correspond with our own—wonderful; but if they were directed elsewhere, as in this case, our responsibility lay in encouraging, affirming, and supporting his interest.

If we are to be authentic stewards of potential and live in the world of possibility and trust in the connectivity of humankind and the rich variety of social ministries sponsored by the Catholic Church and people of goodwill, then we have a moral obligation to encourage great generosity toward that which both makes a donor deeply satisfied and glad and fulfills a social good. I vastly preferred that this donor make a major investment in the Cristo Rey or Nativity/San Miguel networks of schools, for example, than for him to make a perfunctory, modest gift to our campaign and nothing to the educational efforts benefiting the poorest children in our cities. Leaders and development directors must be on the lookout for opportunities to excite the philanthropic imaginations of philanthropists even at the expense of their own dollar goals and campaign plans. If we all did this, there would be vastly more generosity in the world, supporting all manner of noble, compelling ministries and initiatives aimed at making this a better world, a less violent world, a more equitable world, a less malnourished world. The task is to recognize our place connected to the greater collective effort of philanthropy and inspire and encourage great generosity. Everyone wins.

> "I long to see a radical shift in philanthropy that will come to characterize the 21st century. That is, a reclaiming of the root meaning of philanthropy: love of what it means to be human."
>
> —Valaida Fullwood

Frequently we make the mistake that there is a fixed pie of philanthropic generosity to be parceled out to the most worthy charities. Even if this were true, we are only looking at a fraction of a sliver of that pie. Expand the slice! Expand the pie!

Listening carefully and attentively to our prospective donor, seeing him as a subject, not an object, ministering to him, having an open, pastoral heart, and encouraging him in his primary philanthropic passion was the right thing to do. On the MetroNorth commuter train back to New Haven, Fr. Bob and I discussed at length what I had done. He agreed with me and was grateful we had so many educational opportunities to bring to his attention. Fr. Bob was not possessive and guarded about prospective donors. We were engaged, attentive, responsive, and encouraging. We treated him the way we would want to be treated. We were pastoral, first and foremost. We had vowed that our development effort would always be informed and guided by our shared spirituality and conducted according to the very Christian virtues we were trying to emulate. And so at the risk of delaying our fundraising efforts and missing a chance for a new pledge or gift, we encouraged the prospective donor to explore how he might help poor children in the greater New York City area. As a close friend of mine once said, "God's voice is always the voice of encouragement, never discouragement." We left materially poorer but spiritually richer.

And as is so often the case with morality tales, this one had an unexpected, beautiful happy ending. We kept in touch with him, effecting introductions to others from the world of philanthropy who shared his particular interest. And we watched him grow in fulfillment as he invested in superbly run local schools serving the poor. One day he called to let us know that he had decided to leave Saint Thomas More Chapel several million dollars in his will. To this day we are convinced that this was due in large measure to the integrity he saw in us, in how explicit we were about putting his philanthropic desire ahead of our wants. Generosity begets generosity. Everyone benefits.

9

Passionate Investment and Radical Detachment

We had reserved the entire day on our calendars, months in advance, in order to travel to meet with prospective donors.

This was a necessary discipline. Time is the rarest of commodities. With multiple competing claims for our attention exacerbated by increased personal and professional responsibilities, we treated the future dates reserved for travel as inviolable and sacrosanct.

This explains why on this particular occasion with only one confirmed appointment in Boston, despite every effort to secure more, we resisted the temptation to postpone the trip.

The two-and-a-half-hour drive from New Haven was pleasant and constructive. We were amiable partners in our multimillion dollar campaign with a bold and transformative vision. Time spent together in transit meant we were protected from the vagaries of interruption and distraction. It helped that we enjoyed each other's company immensely.

Arriving with precision, we were permitted thirty minutes of our prospective donor's time. He responded positively to the vision, approved of the approach, and commended the accomplishments to date. And he agreed to a financial commitment. We thanked him for his time and support and took our leave.

Even before our seat belts were securely buckled, a philosophical debate commenced. Was this really the best use of this day? Would we not have been better served by canceling the appointment and rescheduling on a day when we had more people to see? What possible good would come of this day's efforts when we could have used the time catching up on correspondence, paperwork, and other administrative duties? Now look at all this traffic!

To restore an atmosphere of conviviality and proper perspective, I resorted to a familiar tactic. I reminded my beloved colleague that he wasn't always an old curmudgeon; he was once a young curmudgeon. Having succeeded in making him laugh, I pointed out that we had just been given the promise of a financial contribution to the campaign, and while it constituted a tiny fraction of the campaign's ambitious goal, it was nevertheless a generous gift freely given in support of our mission. Furthermore, had the contribution been the very first commitment of the entire campaign, it would have been uncontested cause for immediate and joyful celebration. Perspective is crucial but can cut both ways.

Fearing the return trip would seem unusually long if we persisted in the pros and cons of having kept our resolve to embark on the journey in the first place, we knew the matter needed to be settled and put to rest.

The Dalai Lama has instructed that if one's intentions are sound, some good will always come of one's efforts. We needed to trust in this. All we could do, I argued, is our very best, bringing our full selves to the pursuit, with tenacity and confidence and fidelity to purpose. We had an urgent mission, compelling vision, sound goals, and effective strategies. It was working; our progress and accomplishments were measurable and evident. We could not afford to be seduced into postponing our plans or giving up prematurely, sidetracked by disappointment. As long as our intentions were sound and we began every day ready to embrace hard work and effort, some good would always come.

The key was in trusting that our efforts would be fruitful without insisting we knew what constituted a successful result. Too often we expect if we do x, then y will be the optimal outcome. Not only do we imagine the optimal outcome, we ascribe timelines and defining characteristics to it. And when that outcome in all the specificity we have dictated does not materialize, we are discouraged.

What if we are thinking too small?

The example of our trip to Boston is instructive. For what we could neither have known nor predicted was that soon after our journey to Boston, our new donor encountered a classmate from Yale, and inspired by our informative, if brief, visit, proceeded to serve as a most enthusiastic narrator and advocate of our efforts.

This classmate, intrigued by what he had heard, invited the Catholic chaplain and me to visit him when we were next in New York City where he lived. And thus began what would become a deeply meaningful and caring friendship leading to a re-markably unusual gift. Years later, he informed us that he wanted to leave one quarter of his entire

"By detachment I mean that you must not worry whether the desired result follows from your action or not, so long as your motive is pure, your means correct."

—Mahatma Gandhi

estate to the Catholic Center at Yale, a magnificent testamentary gift, but that was not all. Having conducted his due diligence prior to formalizing such a generous offer, he said, "If you need the money now to meet the construction costs as the new center is built, I will advance all that you need—interest-free—to meet those payments, obviating the need for a commercial loan and concomitant interest. As pledge payments from other alumni arrive over time, you can simply return what I have advanced to you so that I can continue to invest it on the center's behalf as a gift in my will."

Extraordinary.

Impossible to predict.

Magnanimous.

Retrospectively, perhaps no trip taken on behalf of Catholic life at Yale was ever more consequential than that drive to Boston so long ago. Then again, rarely do we have the capacity to trace the intricate paths that lead from purposeful and faithful action to magnificent blessing. We can only trust in a future of beneficence and grace that bears signs of the seeds of sound intentions. We can only commit, over and over again, to "taking the trip," with unwavering fidelity to purpose.

And we can marvel and give thanks that God's imagination is always greater than our own.

Dark Night of the Soul

> God,
> Empty me of all that stands between
>   you and me
>   that I might be filled with
>   your imagination, desire, love, and will.
> Help me to be an effective instrument
>   of all that you intend.

I conceived of this prayer the hard way: alone, demoralized, afraid, misunderstood, in a seemingly impossible situation. I literally could not see my way out or through the terrible dilemma we experienced. On the one hand, we were radically committed to the development effort, but as the expectations and goals grew with every small step of success, nothing we did seemed to be executed well enough or fast enough.

We were more than halfway through the capital campaign. The magnitude of responsibility grew in inverse proportion to the faith others had in its success. The pressure was unbearable. With incremental success came exponential expectations. The stakes grew, the goalpost moved, the point of complete achievement seemed further and further out of reach with dire concomitant consequences if never attained.

I dedicated every waking moment to the development effort, cultivating a joyful, confident disposition, rejecting the seduction of cynicism. But every night, exhausted, I was miserable by the burden of the sacrifice and the loneliness of having faith in the effort's value and confidence in its eventual success.

One night I stayed awake until dawn, anxiety coursing through my veins, pondering my dilemma. The easy solution was to quit. I could leave in peace, resume my carefree life, turn my attention to other pursuits and people. It was an attractive choice but not a faithful one. And I knew it. I had accepted responsibility for the role not as a job but as a vocation. I was covenant-bound, hence the excruciating quandary.

There are two striking passages in the Palm Sunday readings that point to the tremendous anguish Jesus experienced and to his radical surrender to God's intent. The first, from the second reading (Phil 2:7-8), is that Christ "emptied himself . . . coming in human likeness . . . he humbled himself, becoming obedient to death, even death on a cross." And the second, from Mark's gospel (14:36), is the anguish of Jesus in the garden when his disciples had fallen asleep and he entreats God to "take this cup away" but ultimately surrenders to what God's will would be, not his own.

The night of my own torment, I called to mind these passages: Christ's emptying of himself for the sake of fidelity and love; Christ's agony in the garden; Christ alone, abandoned, frightened, entreating God to present another option; Christ's relinquishment of self to God's intent.

And I begged God to help me be likewise faithful, to empty my own self of all that stood between God and me, to radically surrender to what God intended.

But how to discern what God intends? Clearly it was not merely a matter of intellectual assent. In feverish prayer this dark night of my soul, I was presented a choice: quit or recommit. What made recommitting the compelling option was the confidence I had that if I did, the potential in its most ambitious imaginings would come to full fruition. But there was a price. I had to surrender completely and give up all desire of anything for myself. In essence God's deal was this: recommit to the project but give up the hope and expectation to be recognized, compensated, thanked, vindicated, or loved for my dedication to the project. Then, God would ensure that the effort would come to full fruition.

Radical surrender. It was all the more impossible because it wasn't fair. And yet, as I sweated it out in my own garden of Gethsemane, alone and frightened, I knew that I wanted other people's lives to be blessed by the project more than I wanted the immediate gratification of vindication for my own fidelity, hard work, and confidence in the project's value. It was painful and honest prayer, intellectual, physical, and emotional at once. For hours I pondered each deeply human, authentic desire, reluctant to give up any of them.

And finally I did. It was a complete stripping away of ego. And the moment I surrendered the last of these desires, I was flooded with a deep and all-consuming peace. I remember actually laughing with relief and saying to God before finally heading for bed, "I am completely in your hands, and I don't know how on earth you are going to solve this mess and make it all have a happy ending, but I trust you completely and have no doubt that all will be well."

Once I surrendered, those desires held no more power over me. I was completely free of distraction to attend to the work. In time, the development effort was a success, a magnificent one, in fact. And most curious of all, everything I had so painstakingly relinquished was ultimately given to me. It was just that all of those things no longer had a claim to my soul and psyche. I was neither possessed nor obsessed with any of those human desires. I was detached and free. And when at the end of it all appreciation, gratitude, compensation, even love and understanding were shared with me, I was able to receive them freely, with surprise, detachment, curiosity, and delight.

It is helpful to reflect on what it is that God is asking you to surrender. Of what do you need to empty yourself in order to be filled with God's imagination, desire, love, and will? What causes your heart the greatest anguish? Of what are you most afraid and most afraid to lose?

Can you trust that in your greatest suffering, at your most vulnerable and frightened, God is fully present to you, offering you the promise of new life?

On Dying

One of the final blessings Tom Golden gave to us was the invitation to accompany him in his illness and to be present to him as he lay dying. We were given a last and lasting gift of intimacy, soulful discussion, and heartfelt, mutual expressions of love and gratitude.

Soon after his passing, I sat in rapt attention when on a gentle evening, as relatives and friends gathered in familiar pose and conversation on our porch, the subject turned rather suddenly to the best way to die. The question was specific in its intensity. "How would you like to experience your own death?"

Over bottles of wine and candlelight we took turns articulating the pros and cons of the myriad ways any one of us might experience our own death. It was not entirely morbid. One friend suggested that she would like to die suddenly and quickly, without warning, ideally after a spectacularly joyful celebration. An-other suggested that he would prefer to have as much time as possible with the knowledge of a terminal illness in order to make amends, to thank his

"The art of living well and the art of dying well are one."

—Epicurus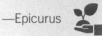

friends and family, and to be intentional about giving away every-thing he possessed. Another was certain that dying in her sleep, peacefully, at the end of a long life is the most desirable. And so the conversation ensued until the oldest at the table, my father, turned to the youngest at the table, my thirteen-year-old daughter.

"Sophie, you have been very quiet and very attentive, but you have not yet volunteered an answer. Do you have an opinion on the way you would most like to die?"

Everything became still and silent. I held my breath. Too late I wondered if she was too young for such deep, existential, potentially distressing discourse. Perhaps she had never seriously considered the matter.

Now at the center of everyone's attention, aware that a response was being asked of her, she replied very simply, "Yes. I hope I die saving someone else's life."

10

New Life

My professor and spiritual director, Margaret Farley, a Religious Sister of Mercy, often reminded her students when they became discouraged about the church to "remember what it is you most love about the church and membership in it. Name it. Claim it." I have never forgotten this advice. I am grateful for what I most love about the church and membership in it. My list is long. Acknowledging what I most love about the church helps me to stay focused on its authenticity, holiness, and potential; allows me to discern what is ignoble; and gives me a roadmap to proceed tirelessly to promote the conditions for the church to manifest its life-giving qualities and correct and make amends for its sinful qualities.

One of the core tenets of Christianity is the centrality of the paschal mystery: that out of Christ's suffering and death comes new life.

Many philanthropists and founders of new initiatives and faith-based nonprofits are motivated by gratitude for the blessings they have received. And out of this stance of gratitude they want to pay it forward, love God back, and attend to the needs of others.

Often, however, it is personal tragedy, loss, or great suffering that inspires a person to be radically other-centered and generous. Each time I encounter this, I am struck by how authentically the person is living out her own paschal mystery. I marvel at the fact that we may never know why there is such tragedy, suffering, loss, and anguish in the world and may never find meaning in such desolation, but we can always find meaning in how we respond.

My earliest example of this was learning about how the Raskob Foundation came into existence. John and Helena had thirteen children. Their son Bill was widely regarded as the heir apparent to John's business dealings. He showed an early aptitude, was charismatic and charming and smart.

"You cannot protect yourself from sadness without protecting yourself from happiness."

—Jonathan Safran Foer

He cared about others. He was one of very few Catholics to attend Yale University in the 1920s and ten months before he was due to graduate, he was tragically killed in a car accident. The family was devastated.

John and Helena were advised in their grief to take what would have been Bill's inheritance and set up a small philanthropic foundation in his memory. The goal of the Bill Raskob Foundation, that still exists to this day, is to provide small no-interest loans to students to allow them to complete their studies and earn their degrees from higher educational institutions.

Their positive experience of honoring the memory of their beloved son in this manner led them years later to establish the much more consequentially endowed Raskob Foundation for Catholic Activities. Nothing can ameliorate the excruciating pain of losing a child, but John and Helena experienced their own paschal mystery by taking their grief and converting it into a blessing for others through the instruments of the Bill Raskob Foundation and the Raskob Foundation for Catholic Activities. Almost a century later, thousands of deserving students have been afforded the opportunity to complete their degrees with no-interest loans, and Catholic ministries all over the world have been supported financially. Out of suffering and death can come new life.

On a personal level, with reverence and surprise, I trace the long thread of history and give thanks for the lives of Helena and John and Bill, for the invitation to be part of the Raskob Foundation, for the exposure to the global church it affords, and for the imprint of their legacy on my own character and conscience. I think of Bill, almost a century later, as I walk through Old Campus at Yale, where my son is now a sophomore. I am struck by the friendship of John Raskob and Fr. T. Lawrason Riggs, Yale's first Catholic chaplain, and their collaboration in helping to found *Commonweal Magazine*. I am impressed by their advocacy of the role of the laity and the lay-clergy collaboration they evinced decades before Vatican II. I imagine how bemused they would be that John's great-granddaughter and the seventh Catholic chaplain at Yale embodied their values and aspirations.

On several trips to Washington, DC, we accessed the journals Fr. Riggs meticulously kept throughout his life, now housed at the Library of Congress. He never wanted a private club for Catholics at Yale, even going so far as to resist the classification of Newman Center to describe what Saint Thomas More at Yale properly was, that is, a Catholic Center at a non-Catholic college or university. Fr. Riggs thought it connoted a private club for Catholics, and he wanted a center of Catholic intellectual and spiritual life fully integrated into the university he loved. Like John Raskob, Fr. Riggs was prescient. It didn't matter that he was one of only eight Catholics to graduate from Yale in 1910. He imagined a time when the percentage and number of Catholics at Yale would be much greater. I wish that these visionary, generous men could see Catholic life at Yale now, but that is the curious, wonderful thing about prophets: they do not need to live to see that they were right to invest so fully in a future not their own.

The Get In Touch Foundation

One of my closest friends, my soul-sister, a beautiful, vibrant, vivacious woman, Mary Ann Wasil, is a ten-year breast cancer survivor currently living with metastatic disease. When she was first diagnosed with breast cancer, she responded by taking what was a very difficult experience and converting it to be a blessing for others. She did this in many ways, including inviting photojournalist Christopher Capozziello to document her health journey without even knowing where that journey would lead. Mary Ann had been a model and was accustomed to being photographed. What dismayed her as she consulted with her oncologist, surgeons, and healing team was that there were few pictures of the whole person, only rather clinical images of body parts in various stages of healing and reconstruction. She wanted to know what life would be and look like during and after breast cancer. Above all, she wanted to take her suffering, anxiety, and anguish and transform it in some

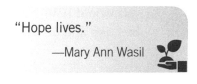

"Hope lives."

—Mary Ann Wasil

fashion so that others would benefit. In addition to the beautiful and evocative photo exhibit, "Diary of Healing," that tours the country and allows viewers to record their reflections in journals that accompany the exhibit, Mary Ann is the founder, president, and CEO of the Get In Touch Foundation.

The Get In Touch Foundation is a global breast health educational nonprofit that teaches girls in grades 5 through 12 the importance of and how to do a breast self-exam, to understand their bodies and be advocates for their own health. In the midst of treatments and tests, raising three exquisite children, and running the Foundation, Mary Ann has provided countless hours of support and encouragement to other survivors. Mary Ann lives with intention and purpose. And when the women and men she counsels and comforts seek to be reassured that there is life after cancer, my vivacious, joyful friend replies, "Is there life after cancer? There's life right in the middle of cancer!" Grace.

The National Leadership Roundtable on Church Management

A major point of emphasis in our effort to raise money for Catholic campus ministry at Yale was the elevation of Catholic intellectual life on campus. Proudly we revealed to alumni and prospective donors that we were elevating and celebrating Catholic intellectual discourse, taking the topics of the day, illuminating them from the perspective of faith, and inviting students into a dynamic discussion about the relevance and role of faith. Halfway through the Saint Thomas More capital campaign, quite dramatically and suddenly, and most certainly devastatingly, the topic of the day was the Catholic Church's sexual abuse crisis.

Nothing in our lifetime was more damaging, discrediting, heartbreaking, or shocking about the church than these revelations.

It would have been tempting to admit our lack of culpability in the crisis and do nothing. Tempting, but not faithful. We knew that to do nothing is to be complicit. Instead we hosted a three-day conference entitled "Governance, Accountability, and the Future of the Catholic Church" to examine the underlining conditions that may have contributed to the crisis, with a view to making a meaningful and positive

"Poor management of school systems issues in poor education. Poor management of courts of law leads to inferior justice. Poor management of corporations results in low returns for investors. Poor management of the church blunts accomplishment of the church's sacred mission."

—Donald J. Monan, SJ

contribution to our church. The conference was held in March of 2003. We hosted 500 people over three days, featuring thirty nationally recognized speakers, including then Bishop (now Cardinal) Wuerl from Pittsburgh who opened the conference with an important keynote, followed by Peter Steinfels, religion editor at the *New York Times*. The subject matter was wrenching, and yet everyone left hopeful. We all belonged to the church. This was *our* church, understanding the problems at hand was the first step, committing to being part of the solution was the second step, acting on that commitment was the third step. Participants left with the sense that it was possible, even if very difficult, to help call the church to greater levels of accountability and holiness. We could all play a role in making a positive contribution. And clearly the laity had much to offer, particularly in the areas of management of human and financial resources, contemporary best practices, and solutions to complex temporal challenges facing church leaders.

The seminal papers from the conference were edited by Francis Oakley and Bruce Russett, and *Governance, Accountability, and the Future of the Catholic Church* was published. It was a significant contribution to the future health of the church in the United States, and the community of Saint Thomas More Chapel was justifiably proud of the beneficial role it had played.

Three months later in Memphis, Tennessee, on June 7, 2003, I met Geoff Boisi, who delivered an impeccable keynote to a prominent group of Catholic philanthropists convened by FADICA on the same theme, with remarkably consistent conclusions and with the same heartfelt motivation. Geoff wanted to help our church overcome what was properly understood as a managerial crisis. I was spellbound by his presentation, the content, the delivery, and the respect he commanded by his presence, leadership, and obvious dedication. I entreated him to meet with trustees and colleagues from Yale in order that we could collaborate to strengthen the church.

The first of these meetings took place at the home of Fay Vincent, a member of the board of trustees of Saint Thomas More Chapel. Geoff and Fay already knew each other, but this was a chance for Fr. Bob and Geoff to meet and for the four of us to discuss how Saint Thomas More Chapel and the conference on church governance we had just hosted could be helpful in a much broader contribution to the church. Fay had been hugely influential in persuading the board of Saint Thomas More Chapel to host the conference and was the conference's major benefactor. There is nothing as thrilling as being in the company of visionaries—leaders who care deeply, who are smart, experienced, unafraid, and committed to making a meaningful difference. And we were surrounded by baseball memorabilia, treasures given to Fay when he was commissioner of Major League Baseball.

The best of Vatican II is personified in Geoff Boisi. He could have done anything with his time in this last decade of so much challenge for the church. An extraordinary leader and visionary, world-renowned for his financial and investment acumen, past chair of Boston College, member of the Papal Foundation, cofounder of Mentor, wonderful husband, father, and grandfather, Geoff deserved some time off. But when his church was in crisis, he did everything possible to effect healing and reconciliation. Exercising baptismal responsibility—not only taking his faith to make the world better but taking his faith to make our church better—Geoff founded the National Leadership Roundtable on Church Management.

The founding board of directors of the National Leadership Roundtable on Church Management, recruited and inspired by Geoff, was an all-star cast of ordained, religious, and lay leaders. The directors convened for the first time in Washington, DC, on July 11, 2005. Included among the founding board members was Lieutenant General James Dubik, a three-star general of the U.S. Army, and Geoff's eventual successor as chair.

It was a grand experiment that had never been tried anywhere in the world before that moment. It was also a perfect example of stewardship on the part of all of the baptized to care well for what has been entrusted to the church and to recognize the enormous potential before us.

The Leadership Roundtable is an exceptional network of senior-level leaders from all walks of life, all of whom are Catholic and committed to making a meaningful contribution to the church. It is comprised of ordained, religious, and lay leaders from a diverse composite of sectors, industries, geographical regions, and experiences. Senior-level executive members come from the corporate, nonprofit, philanthropic, financial, communications, executive recruiting, marketing, academic, and other sectors, including the church itself. When the Roundtable was first created, twenty-four national Catholic networks whose own missions had a bearing on ours were identified, and the chair or executive director was invited to be a member. It is extremely important that we not duplicate efforts, that we collaborate whenever possible, and that we not reinvent what has already been created but rather analyze whether we can build on such solutions, practices, and protocols.

These women and men bring with them decades of successful leadership, problem-solving ability, managerial expertise, financial acumen, sophisticated command of technology, and capabilities in marketing and communications. They value the church and want it to be strengthened. They yearn to contribute to the restoration of trust that had been so painfully shattered by the sexual abuse crisis. They want to help usher in a new day of ethics, transparency, accountability, best practices, and excellence. They highlight the particular skill and expertise laypeople have at their disposal and the importance of recognizing and inviting such expertise to strengthen the church.

Catholics are no longer solely an immigrant population in the United States. Thanks in part to the GI Bill and access to quality education, Catholics have risen to levels of affluence and influence and now count among the highest echelons of leadership in every sector and industry. Witness the U.S. Supreme Court with five Catholic justices. Given such vast leadership expertise, laity have been a wholly underutilized resource in the church. For far too long, laity were passive, complicit in our passivity in the very clericalism that would later be decried as a fundamental condition contributing to the sexual abuse crisis and managerial handling of that crisis. Why were such smart, opinionated, talented, self-possessed laymen and laywomen so reluctant to speak up or out or to offer their particular expertise to strengthen their parish, diocese, or favorite Catholic ministry? If there is any grace that came from the sexual abuse crisis in the United States, it is that it roused laity out of our lethargy and enkindled a desire to act on our convictions that a better managed church, a more transparent church, and a more accountable church would be more effective at its mission, more faithful to its purpose.

Ordained and religious church leaders had rarely looked to laity for more than financial contributions. To ignore their considerable command of managerial expertise and problem-solving capability when it is clear this is what the church needs and can significantly benefit from is to be a poor steward of one of the most valuable assets of all.

Geoff knew this and set about harnessing it for the good of the church.

A few extremely important charisms and strategic guidelines were identified and put into place as the Leadership Roundtable took shape.

Exclusive focus on temporal affairs

First, it would never be the role of the Leadership Roundtable to weigh in on any doctrinal matters. The membership is theologically and politically diverse, across the full spectrum. Whether a parish, ministry, or apostolate is considered progressive or orthodox, liberal or conservative, is only a use of imperfect terms that in this case don't pertain to the mission of the Roundtable. Simply stated, if any Catholic entity takes seriously the managerial best practices being advocated, its mission will be strengthened and more effective. This means, also, that no recalcitrant church leader can ever accuse the Roundtable of not being faithful to the magisterium, or not being "truly Catholic." Our strength is in providing particular managerial, problem-solving expertise, and best practices that serve to create the conditions for openness, accountability, transparency, ethics, exemplary human resource management, and effective utilization of technology, marketing, and communications. Furthermore, although often borrowing from examples of best practices proven effective in corporations, large secular nonprofits, the military, and even other faith traditions, everything we adapt for specific utility in the Catholic Church is first vetted through the lens of canon law to ensure canonically compliant contemporary best practices.

Positive and laudatory

Second, we are intentionally positive and laudatory. Although it is imperative that we know the extent of the challenges at hand, our job is not to embarrass or humiliate anyone or to draw public attention to examples of mismanagement. Our job is to work with church leaders to identify unmet needs and work toward solutions. Many times throughout our first decade of service to the church we heard the prediction that "the next wave of scandal will be in the area of church finances." If this were to be true, we wanted to equip bishops, pastors, and provincials with the tools needed to ensure full financial accountability and standards for excellence to militate against the deleterious effects of malfeasance, ignorance, inadequate systems, and vulnerable financial protocols.

Furthermore, whenever we identify an example of best managerial practice that already exists in the church, and there are many, we draw positive attention to it. We celebrate it, elevate it, and argue that it is worthy of dissemination and emulation. From the very beginning the Roundtable has offered best practices awards to a variety of church entities honoring examples of effective management. Recipients have included Cardinal Sean O'Malley and the Archdiocese of Boston for the Archdiocese of Boston Financial Transparency Project; the episcopal leaders of the Gulf of Mexico for their leadership in rebuilding the church after Hurricane Katrina and introducing best managerial practices as a core component in the rebuilding effort; Women & Spirit: Catholic Sisters in America; Center for Social Concerns at the University of Notre Dame; Bishop Dale Melczek and the Diocese of Gary for commitment to implementing the Standards for Excellence; Catholic Charities USA; and many more.

Convening capability, candor, and charity

One of the greatest strengths of the Roundtable is its convening power. Whatever the issue identified by church leaders, we are able to identify the best thought leaders within our network and beyond it, ensuring diversity of perspective and expertise to foster entrepreneurial approaches and innovation. Our ground rules are candor and charity. All ideas and analyses are welcome. Egos are checked at the door. When bishops and executives meet, they have far more in common than not, but neither has the full understanding of what it is like to be the other. The benefit of the doubt is always extended, presumption is accorded that all who participate in these deliberations have the very best interests in mind and heart for the church. And we adhere to the maxim first proffered by Charles Edward Montague: "Imagine how much can be accomplished when nobody cares who gets the credit."

Think big and never give up

When needs are identified for which there are no or only inadequate solutions, we set to work on creating solutions that are effective with large impact. When we encounter resistance to the solutions or even to an acknowledgment that the problem exists, we are polite in the face of the resistance but never stop working to make a meaningful contribution. An example of this is the following:

In many dioceses fifty years ago, a newly ordained priest had the benefit of living for as many as twenty or twenty-five years in a rectory community with other seasoned, experienced priests. Much of the new priest's formation occurred in such parish settings, with mentors and real parish experience under the leadership of the pastor or senior curate. It might be as many as twenty-five years before the priest would be assigned as pastor of a parish. Today priests who are ordained as little as eighteen months are named pastor and given not one but often two or three parishes, sometimes with schools. These newly ordained priests are expected to manage, without any other priests to help or mentor them and without having had the benefit of a single course in management, finance, or human resource development in the seminary. Their budgets can be in the category of many millions of dollars.

Our observation was that we were unwittingly setting these good men up for failure. Tom Healey, a founding member of the board of the Leadership Roundtable and a paragon of philanthropic dedication, spearheaded our focused response to this pressing challenge. Our first approach was to appeal to the seminary rectors to revise the curriculum to include basic management of people and finances. Their initial response was that the curriculum was already too full, that nothing could be subtracted to make room for the managerial courses, that seminarians did not discern vocations to become managers but priests. It simply could not be done without adding another year to an already long seminary formation.

Our response was one of understanding and empathy, and yet we could not in good conscience let this growing, urgent need continue to go unmet. With Tom as chair of this effort, Fr. Paul Holmes as director, and support from Lilly Endowment, we formed a team of diverse thought leaders and proposed an interim solution while we waited for what we knew would be inevitable: managerial courses in the seminary curriculum and ongoing formation and training. We created a six-day retreat for new pastors entitled Toolbox for Pastoral Management. Thirty to thirty-five pastors from all over the country attend each one. There is evening prayer, Mass and fellowship, and every day faculty, expert in key managerial aspects, teach. Six days is not enough, of course, but the pastors begin to develop a vocabulary for speaking credibly about this aspect of their leadership and are introduced into an online community, CatholicPastors.org, for ongoing support, access to managerial best practices, and a network of peers.

Standards for Excellence

Many bishops, provincials, and pastors say to us, "We want to ensure that the way we are stewarding our finances and caring for our employees reflects contemporary best managerial practices, but how do we know if we are in fact doing so?"

Before creating a template from scratch, we scanned the horizon and found a valuable resource that was being utilized to great effect in secular nonprofits in the States. It was called *Standards for Excellence: An Ethics and Accountability Code for the Nonprofit Sector*. When we looked at it through the lens of the managerial challenges facing the Catholic Church, we realized that had this been implemented and adhered to by the church we could have avoided much of the heartache and scandal of the past decades. We entered into a licensing agreement with the creators of the Standards, translated them into specific utility in a Catholic context, vetted it entirely through the lens of canon law, and are now disseminating it throughout the church in the United States.

Our Catholic Standards for Excellence is a comprehensive set of fifty-five best management practices compiled from the various areas of temporal life relevant to the good stewardship of Catholic religious communities, parishes, dioceses, and nonprofits. The program includes a cohesive set of downloadable resources corresponding to each of the fifty-five standards providing essential information and tools helpful in implementing each of the management practices.

The Catholic parishes, dioceses, religious communities, schools, universities, and organizations that are implementing the Catholic Standards for Excellence experience greater impact from their ministerial efforts, more engagement by the laity, and more human and financial resources to serve the mission of the church. Trust is restored and nurtured. Systems of checks and balances and accountability are put in place.

Pooled Investment Initiative

The members of the Leadership Roundtable think big and don't shy away from complex challenges or high-impact solutions. They identify potential and work to bring it to fruition. An example is the promotion of a pooled investment initiative that allows the endowments of religious communities, dioceses, Catholic colleges, hospitals, nonprofits, and other Catholic entities to come together to form one large client in order to access the best investment opportunities and investors and have a far more consequential return on investment.

Undergirding this opportunity is a strong and contemporary commitment to socially responsible investment that ensures to the fullest extent possible that positive screens are in place to care for the social responsibility of investment and to have a positive influence on secular investors.

Young Adult Leadership

Another example of a challenge we believe to be urgent and necessary is to encourage young adult leadership in the church.

Every young adult in the Raskob family knows what it is like to be encouraged to assume roles of leadership in the Raskob Foundation even when we are teenagers. From the moment we are eighteen and formally invited into membership of the foundation and throughout our twenties, we are encouraged to represent the family at national Catholic gatherings, to make site visits to potential grantees, to serve as chairs of committees, to speak publicly, and to stand for election to the board of trustees of the Raskob Foundation. It is perhaps the single most effective defining characteristic of the Raskob Foundation: the youngest members of the family are the ones most encouraged in genuine leadership opportunities. The consequence of this habit is a far greater investment in the life of the foundation and in the life of the church. We don't wait until members of the family are well into their fifties or sixties to invite them to play a meaningful role in the foundation. If that were our practice, there is no doubt in our minds that most members of the family would by then politely decline any meaningful participation.

Years later, this insight would prove relevant when Geoff Boisi, Fr. Bob, and I embarked on a series of conversations about why the church was losing so many young adults and what could be done to stem the exodus.

For decades, leaders of the church in the United States have observed that many young adult Catholics enjoy a positive experience of the church while they are in college, either because they attend a Catholic university or because they attend a secular university that has a vibrant Catholic campus ministry. Catholic students note the exceptional liturgies, relevant homilies, student participation, opportunities for service, and attention to helping them develop a mature adult faith that is both cognitive and affective. These are the best-educated generations of Catholics the United States has ever had, and as soon as they leave campus their participation in the church plummets.

For a very long time, leaders have observed and lamented this. The conclusion has always been the same: "We know that many young adults will drift away from the church for a period of time following commencement. They graduate and move to a new city to start their first job, and their neighborhood parish has few single young adults, the homilies seem aimed more at the elderly or families with young children. We know that the church risks losing them for a time, but they will come back when they get married, have a child or experience a personal crisis."

I have heard this all of my life. Geoff and Fr. Bob were the first to say, "That is not a good strategic plan." And so they set about finding a solution. Their first observation was that the prediction was no longer true, if it ever had been. Catholics were not coming back to the church. For one thing, they were not necessarily marrying other Catholics or raising their children Catholic. The long-term impact was that the church was losing its best-educated generation of members. From a Leadership Roundtable perspective, this was a human resource challenge of enormous consequence. From a campus ministry perspective, this was a disheartening reality. How to prepare college students for active engagement in the church and ensure that the church would be welcoming and receptive to young adults when they graduated from college?

From a practical standpoint, we wondered how we could harness the vibrancy of the Catholic Center at Yale and the problem-solving capabilities of the Leadership Roundtable and create a curriculum and framework for preparing college students for meaningful leadership in the church immediately upon graduation.

To accomplish this, we convened leaders from across the country whose expertise was in young adult ministry, campus ministry, human resource development, leadership development, theology, canon law, ecclesiology, and sociology. Over a period of eighteen months a young adult leadership formation program was created called ESTEEM—Engaging Students to Enliven the Ecclesial Ministry.

It was piloted on six campuses from Stanford to Yale and prevailed upon campus ministers to invite "the best and brightest" young adult Catholics to apply for the yearlong program. An opening retreat, with curriculum prepared for sessions throughout the year, would expose students to ecclesiology, canon law, Catholic social teaching, intellectual, sacramental, and liturgical life and leadership formation. At the end of the year all participating students would meet for a national capstone conference and commissioning ceremony. Each student is paired with a mentor, a local leader whose field of expertise most closely aligns with the professional aspirations of the student. Mentors are on hand throughout the year for informal discussion on the role of faith in professional life, in vocational discernment, and in leadership.

The most significant aim of ESTEEM, however, is to equip the student participants for meaningful leadership experience after graduation: by being appointed to a parish pastoral council, a diocesan finance council, or the board of trustees of a Catholic nonprofit. "Be the change you want to see" became our best advice to ESTEEM alumni. Our hope is to imagine and then realize a landscape of participation that has a minimum of two young adults in leadership in every parish, diocesan office, and Catholic charity, from Georgetown University to the local soup kitchen. If young adults see other young adults in meaningful positions of leadership, they know that their voice and perspective matter. Young adults serving on boards will learn from older more experienced trustees, offer their own perspective on ways to strengthen mission, and attract a new generation. Everyone wins.

Letter June 28, 1929

The founding board of directors of the National Leadership Roundtable on Church Management first met in Washington, DC, on July 11, 2005, the result of Geoff Boisi's remarkable dedication, vision, faith, commitment to the church, and tenacity.

And while the concept of the Leadership Roundtable had never been tried anywhere in the world and was therefore a wholly unique experiment, shortly after its founding a letter was discovered. The Raskob family had made available all of John Raskob's papers and archival material to the talented historian and biographer David Farber. In the course of his research on John Raskob, while combing through thousands of documents, David came across a remarkable letter written three quarters of a century before the Leadership Roundtable was founded. Foreshadowing the creation of the Leadership Roundtable, unwittingly laying out its mission statement, John Raskob wrote to the bishop of Oklahoma on June 28, 1929:

> Personally I am a great believer in the church working out some scheme under which the clergy and laity will work together in those things having to do with the temporal side of the church. In other words, I feel that it is important to have the lay people actively interested in the problems of the church in order that they can and may assume responsibilities in an intelligent fashion. The facts are that young men spending their whole lives studying for the priesthood are studying theology and, therefore, are not educated along lines that will enable them, as pastors, to intelligently solve, without assistance things bearing on the material side of the church, such as the building and financing of schools, churches, rectories, etc. etc. The only thing they know how to do is to beg for funds from the altar almost every Sunday and the Catholic layman as a rule, feels that he has little opportunity of helping in anyway except through contributing, in fact most of them are absolutely taught not to speak out, make suggestions and advocate plans, particularly if it happens to meet the opposition of the parish priest. This kind of policy could not work in business. In business every effort is made to get everyone to speak out openly and frankly and honestly and criticize what is being done without fear or favor.

Geoff Boisi had invited me to serve as the first executive director of the Leadership Roundtable, and the Raskob family was one of nine original founders providing capital to form the network. So when David Farber chanced to read this excerpt from this letter to our extended family during an annual Raskob meeting, there was a collective gasp.

Thanks to Geoff and women and men like Geoff, today the church in the United States has at its disposal a remarkable network of committed Catholic leaders from diverse sectors and industries where Catholic philanthropic capital and Catholic intellectual capital is brought together to address complex contemporary temporal challenges. Social entrepreneurial rigor is encouraged for high-impact solutions. Practical, canonically compliant solutions are the result; evangelization of the participating leaders is a byproduct. All assets are utilized, not only financial. Imagination and intellect, expertise and perspective play dominant roles in deliberations. Problems are addressed. Solutions are proposed. Action is taken. Effect is measured. Potential is brought to fruition. And everyone benefits.

Postscript

People who believe it is possible to contribute to and bless the world are the people most equipped to be exceptional fundraisers. People who have faith in the goodness and interconnection of human-kind, who seek transcendence, who yearn for meaning, and who want to be a beneficial presence in the world can make an enormous difference in our communities.

It is notable how many leaders in the nonprofit world—and especially in the faith-based portion of that world—are exceptionally committed to their mission and simultaneously discomforted by the responsibility of raising money. Raising money will always be necessary for true mission effectiveness, expansion, innovation, and impact.

Leaders look for leverage points in order to bring about positive social change efficiently. Changing the framework of how we think about money, philanthropy, and fundraising is a leverage point. These reflections are a start, and I hope a helpful one.

Just as with the spiritual life, habits can be cultivated to allow us to be more generous—and to be catalysts for inspiring *others* to be more generous. These habits correlate well with developing a mature inner life of faith. Therefore it is helpful for people of faith who are committed to worthy missions as leaders in the nonprofit sector to integrate and align such habits, disciplines, and attitudes about fund-raising and philanthropy with those of the spiritual life.

The world is a beautiful and broken place. It needs people like you to make a meaningful difference. Every act of generosity matters.

Every invitation to be generous matters. Reconciliation, peace, human rights, compassion, justice, the alleviation of suffering, the elimination of extreme poverty, care for creation, and universal access to clean water, nourishment, education, and healthcare are all predicated on the conviction that it is possible, even against great odds, to bring such goals to fruition. Imagine this better world, locally, regionally, globally. Imagine that you can make a meaningful, positive impact. You can. And we are all better for it. Thank you for the profound difference your service makes.

"Imagination is everything. It is the preview of life's coming attractions."

—Albert Einstein

Resources

Online

Cristo Rey Network
www.cristoreynetwork.org

ESTEEM (Engaging Students to Enliven the Ecclesial Mission)
www.esteemleadership.org

FADICA (Foundations and Donors Interested in Catholic Activities)
www.fadica.org

Get In Touch Foundation
www.getintouchfoundation.org

National Leadership Roundtable on Church Management
www.TheLeadershipRoundtable.org

Raskob Foundation for Catholic Activities, Inc.
www.rfca.org

Saint Thomas More Catholic Chapel and Center at Yale University
www.stm.yale.edu

Texas Methodist Foundation
www.tmf-fdn.org

Publications

FADICA. *The Catholic Funding Guide*. Washington, DC: FADICA, 2012.
Farber, David. *Everybody Ought to Be Rich: The Life and Times of John J. Raskob, Capitalist*. New York: Oxford University Press, 2013.

Jeavons, Thomas H. and Rebekah Burch Basinger. *Growing Givers Hearts: Treating Fundraising as a Ministry*. San Francisco: Jossey-Bass, 2000.

Nouwen, Henri J. M. *The Spirituality of Fundraising*. Nashville: Upper Room, 2010.

Oakley, Francis and Bruce Russett. *Governance, Accountability and the Future of the Catholic Church*. New York: Continuum, 2003.

Wasil, Mary Ann. *A Diary of Healing: My Intense and Meaningful Life with Cancer*. Bloomington, IN: Balboa, 2013.